SPEAKING ABOUT SCIENCE

Presenting in public is an important career skill for anyone in the sciences, and this practical manual is essential reading for researchers and clinicians who are preparing talks for meetings and academic conferences. The book features step-by-step instruction for creating clear and compelling presentations – from structuring a talk and developing effective PowerPoint slides through delivery before an audience. Color examples of slides and posters from actual presentations are included. The authors also provide tips on answering questions and strategies for handling media inquiries and job interviews.

Scott Morgan and **Barrett Whitener** are professional public speakers and write from their extensive experience designing courses and teaching presentation skills to scientists and medical researchers at the National Institutes of Health and in the private sector. The seven-step process they have developed will help readers become better speakers and ensure success behind the podium.

For more information, visit www.premierepublicspeaking.com.

SPEAKING ABOUT SCIENCE

A MANUAL FOR CREATING CLEAR PRESENTATIONS

Scott Morgan
Premiere Public Speaking, Washington, D.C.

Barrett Whitener
Premiere Public Speaking, Washington, D.C.

CAMBRIDGE
UNIVERSITY PRESS

CAMBRIDGE UNIVERSITY PRESS
Cambridge, New York, Melbourne, Madrid, Cape Town, Singapore, São Paulo

Cambridge University Press
32 Avenue of the Americas, New York, NY 10013-2473, USA

www.cambridge.org
Information on this title: www.cambridge.org/9780521866811

First published 2006

Printed in Hong Kong by Golden Cup

A catalog record for this publication is available from the British Library.

Library of Congress Cataloging in Publication Data

Morgan, Scott, 1961–
Speaking about science : a manual for creating clear presentations / Scott Morgan,
Barrett Whitener.
  p. ;   cm.
Includes bibliographical references and index.
ISBN-13: 978-0-521-86681-1 (hardback)
ISBN-10: 0-521-86681-2 (hardback)
ISBN-13: 978-0-521-68345-6 (pbk.)
ISBN-10: 0-521-68345-9 (pbk.)
1. Communication in science.   2. Science – Vocational guidance.
3. Science – Congresses.   4. Public speaking. [DNLM: 1. Health Occupations.
2. Speech.   3. Science. W 21 M849s 2006]   I. Whitener, Barrett, 1960–   II. Title.
Q223.M67   2006
501′.4 – dc22   2006007797

ISBN-13   978-0-521-86681-1 hardback
ISBN-10   0-521-86681-2 hardback

ISBN-13   978-0-521-68345-6 paperback
ISBN-10   0-521-68345-9 paperback

CONTENTS

ACKNOWLEDGMENTS

Thanks to Jim Alexander, Debbie Cohen, Shirley Forehand, Michael Fortis, Brenda Hanning, Matt Holder, Marc Horowitz, Alfred Johnson, Peter Levonian, Mary McCormick, Joan Schwartz, Gloria Seelman and Pat Sokolov.

Special thanks to Eunice Kilpatrick and Daisy Pascualvaca.

The authors would like to acknowledge those who provided the illustrations used in the book:

Golo Ahlensteil
Jennifer Cockrill
Margot Giannetti
Nalin Goonesekere
Christina Han
Larissa Lapteva
Chunyan Liu
Ariel Michelman-Ribiera
Daisy Pascualvaca
Shi Shu
Cynthia Weickert

INTRODUCTION

Thus, it is the communications process which is at the core of the vitality and integrity of science.

– Philip Hauge Abelson

In an age when so much communication is tethered to technology, delivering messages face-to-face has paradoxically become even more vital to professional success. We all have ready access to more information than any of our ancestors did. At the click of a few keys, we can locate reams of facts on any topic under the sun. But although the amount of data available to us has grown, the number of hours in a day has not. Amidst this flood of information, technology can make getting to the *pertinent* bits of data much more challenging. And that is where a good public speaker becomes a priceless commodity. Listening to a clear and concise speaker is still the most time-efficient way to comprehend new information.

Yet even with its known benefits, most of us view addressing a group of people as a dreaded burden. That may be even more the case for scientists. In addition to the concerns that all speakers have, they must present specialized and complex data.

Some of the dread is also due to the fact that the craft of public speaking is not taught properly. For most of us, it was never taught at all. We all have had to learn by painful trial and error. The purpose of this book is to offer a methodical and efficient procedure that can be used to prepare and deliver any talk, to any audience.

Our method builds cumulatively, so we suggest reading the book in sequence the first time, without jumping between topics. We have tried to enhance readability, yet avoid gender bias, by using masculine pronouns for the odd-numbered chapters and feminine pronouns for the even-numbered chapters. Because our primary focus is on scientific talks, most of our examples come from basic research. But the concepts are easily adapted for clinicians, administrators or review talks.

Lastly, these ideas have hardly developed in isolation. We would like to thank the hundreds of clients who have helped us discover the techniques that make a presentation successful. In fact, we think of them as our teachers, and it is an ongoing honor to learn from them.

Scott Morgan
Barrett Whitener

1 THE BASIC PROBLEM WITH ORAL PRESENTATIONS, AND ITS SOLUTION

> Both science and art have to do with ordered complexity.
> – Lancelot Law Whyte, in the *Griffin* (1957)

We often ask our students, "What's wrong with scientific talks?" They invariably respond with variations of: They are boring; they are too complicated; they are hard to follow; the speakers have too much information for the time allowed; they do not recognize the different knowledge levels of the audience; they do not look at the audience; they talk too fast or too softly; they sound bored with their work.

Conversely, we are told that good presentations are clear, concise, and focus on a few key points and that good speakers are enthusiastic and help the audience to become engaged. We have seen many accomplished presenters ourselves, and it is truly inspiring to see science communicated well.

Still, as anyone who has taken the podium has discovered, simply telling oneself, "Be clear" or "Be enthusiastic" rarely assures success. It is easy to despair over not being a "born presenter." Many struggle because they think they are too introverted, are not funny or because English is an alternative language for them. The truth is that there are very few natural presenters, and even they can benefit from technique. One's gregariousness could not matter less in this context; humor is irrelevant to scientific speaking; and nonnative English speakers actually have a few advantages over native English speakers. This is all to say that giving an effective presentation is more a matter of method than of talent.

Writing vs. Speaking

Both authors have learned about public speaking the hard way. Barrett Whitener, for example, used to take the common approach of writing his speeches out verbatim and delivering them from a script. He took the full text to the podium to ensure that nothing important would be left out. In theory, this tactic was reassuring, but in practice, the detailed wording precluded him from making any meaningful contact with the audience.

Regrettably, for many presenters, a talk is essentially a spoken version of the text. Most of us were taught to construct a written essay by using the three-step guideline, "Tell them what you're going to tell them; tell them; and then tell them what you told them." When it comes time to organize a presentation, many speakers automatically adopt the same structure. Yet, it transfers poorly from the page to the podium.

In principle, whenever written words are involved, the *reader* is in full control of the rate, flow and retention of information. If he daydreams while going over a particular passage, he can read it again. If he needs longer to analyze a chart or graph, so be it. There is unlimited time to absorb the information and its import. Moreover, the reader can learn independently. He can start with the abstract before moving on to the data, or vice versa; he might be struck by a photograph and move backward or forward within the article.

The suspension of linear time does not exist in a speaking situation. The *speaker* determines the rate and flow of delivery, and therefore the rate of absorption. But rather than a hindrance, simultaneous learning is public speaking's most useful quality. Live interaction requires the synchronized attention of speaker and audience on the same detail at every moment during a talk. The presenter cannot progress to the next point until he has discussed the current one thoroughly. In addition, the audience gets only one chance to take in the information. That means the speaker must dole out the data in digestible amounts; there is no going back for clarification. But in this subtle exchange, there is a unique opportunity for him and the audience to learn together. The speaker's primary responsibility is to engage the audience's full attention at all times.

A good presentation is essentially the same as a good story. The speaker keeps the audience in sync with him; they are neither ahead of nor too far behind each turn in the narrative. Scientists are aided greatly in this capacity because a clear description of their scientific method is intrinsically engaging. However, the order in which a speaker unveils each piece of information is critical.

A speaker who follows "written structure," for example, often begins a talk with a summary of everything to be covered in it. He might do this via an outline, a handout, or simply a sentence such as, "Today, I will show you how the syntaxin-1 clamp, syntaphilin, controls the SNARE assembly." But in an effort to introduce the topic, he has turned the presentation into a diluted review of data. This arrangement simply divulges too much information too early, without providing the audience with any background or context first. Furthermore, having divulged the end of his story up front, the speaker becomes a passive tour guide and the audience a passive listener. But most importantly, this plan is not good storytelling because it does not reflect the actual research process. Although the scientist may have worked from a hypothesis, he did not know the final outcome when his experimentation began.

Our own misadventures in public speaking, combined with attending thousands of scientific talks, have led us to devise a different model for presentation.

Presentation Structure: The Hour Glass Format

We call it the "The Hour Glass Format" for its shape; this one has two funnels and three chambers (Figure 1.1). The hour glass is a fitting image for the specificity required at certain points (narrow funnels versus wider ones). It provides a visual reference as to which parts should be expressed more broadly, and which parts will need to be explained in relative detail. It also gives a visual impression of the comparative time allocation for each portion, with briefer

1.1

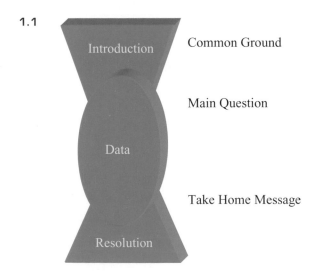

Introduction

Common Ground

Main Question

Data

Take Home Message

Resolution

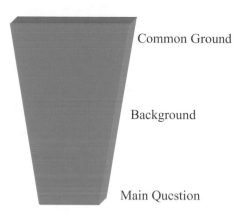

Common Ground

Background

Main Question

1.2

opening and closing segments surrounding the lengthier data section.

To begin breaking down the configuration piece by piece, notice that the widest span of the Introduction (Figure 1.2) is at the top. This represents the initial overture to the audience and should acknowledge their work as well the speaker's – the shared Common Ground. The amount of information covered in the Introduction depends entirely on the composition of the audience. For most talks, the Introduction comprises about 10 percent of the presentation time. The spotlight here should be on concepts, ideas, definitions and goals. The Introduction is essentially a brief background of "the story so far." It ends with the primary focus of the talk: the Main Question.

After the Main Question comes the Data Section, the second portion of the model (Figure 1.3). This section highlights the current work or "the story today." Methodology is presented here, as are any images that help the audience grasp the findings and the course of action. The number of data points that can be comfortably addressed depends on the amount of time allowed for the talk. As an illustration, there are five data points in Figure 1.3. The hour glass shape lengthens in the Data Section to exemplify the larger

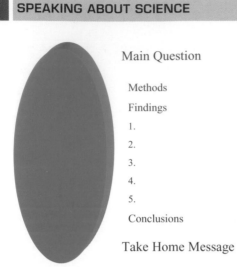

Main Question

Methods

Findings

1.

2.

3.

4.

5.

Conclusions

Take Home Message

1.3

ratio of time needed to describe its contents. Typically, it comprises 75 to 80 percent of the presentation's length. The speaker reviews conclusions before addressing the next key component, the Take Home Message. This is the single most important idea of the talk, one he wants the audience to memorize.

After the Take Home Message, the hour glass widens out again into the Resolution Section, the third and final portion (Figure 1.4). The heart of this section is future directions and studies or "the story ahead." Finally, having a predetermined sentence to conclude the talk, an Exit Line, assures a strong and clear finish.

This is but an overview of the Hour Glass Format – the presentation order of a talk. In the ensuing chapters, we look at the model

1.4

Take Home Message

Future Plans

Exit Line

from a number of perspectives, not only to elaborate on its composition but also to describe how the components interact. Obviously, before the elements are compiled, they must be created. Perhaps surprisingly, however, we suggest approaching preparation in an entirely different sequence from the presentation order.

CHAPTER 1 SUMMARY

A key distinction between writing and speaking is the matter of who controls the rate and flow of information exchange. In an oral presentation, it is the speaker. As a result, the most effective talks follow the principles of good storytelling. The speaker determines the sequence and timing of information so the audience can learn his process in a logical, coordinated and step-by-step fashion.

2 THE FIRST STEPS OF PREPARATION

Theories are nets cast to catch what we call "the world"...We endeavor to make the mesh ever finer and finer.

– Sir Karl Popper, *The Logic of Scientific Discovery* (1959)

Perhaps the following preparation process will look familiar to many speakers: After receiving an invitation to speak, the presenter chooses a title; writes the introduction; searches the data; sorts the slides; and finally, summarizes the conclusion points on a slide.

Scott Morgan used to prepare his talks this way. When he attended a presentation, he would hear the title, introduction, data and conclusion points, and assume they should be prepared in the same order.

But there are several drawbacks to this common strategy. First, there is probably more information to share than available speaking time in which to share it. For a speaker to fit her remarks into the allotted time, she must eliminate some interesting and perhaps essential facts. But perhaps the biggest drawback is that she drowns the talk's central point in the minutiae of excessive detail. As a result, the talk is longer and more detailed than an audience can readily accommodate. No wonder the list of common complaints about talks includes "too complicated" and "too much information."

Mr. Morgan eventually realized that as linear as the preparation process seemed, his own groundwork was actually very different. It was also less time consuming. When invited to speak, he did not begin by writing the title and introduction but instead asked himself, "What do I have to show the audience? What are my best data?"

He had another realization: A week or so after attending a talk, he could recall just one main concept from it. Even when he understood the speaker's work well and took extensive notes, he easily remembered only one major point.

By combining these two discoveries, we have devised a practical strategy for preparing a talk: working backwards.

Working backwards accomplishes an important objective: It builds the presentation outward from the most important point. As opposed to sifting through copious amounts of material in search of the essential idea, the speaker focuses on it from the beginning.

Finding the Take Home Message

As discussed in the previous chapter, the most prominent part of a talk is the data. That is what the audience has come to see and hear. The encapsulation of that data is even more imperative, because it underscores the significance of the facts. Thus, the place to begin preparation is to identify the one concept that reflects the combined import of all the data. This is the one thought the audience should memorize: the main point, the gist, or the Take Home Message. All data for the talk should be selected with this end goal in mind. All images should be designed around it. The Take Home Message guarantees that the speaker clearly states the most important point in the allotted time, while providing a thematic thread for the entire talk.

As the first element prepared, the Take Home Message helps establish what belongs in the talk and what can be set aside. Starting this way is far easier than beginning with the entirety of the subject and eliminating items one by one. In other words, the Take Home Message acts as a filter. From this point on, everything placed in the talk will revolve around it.

The Take Home Message is not the same thing as a speaker's favorite conclusion point. Rather, it is what the conclusion points mean collectively. For example, the following are conclusion points from one presentation:

The combination of RNA interference and micro-array profiling is useful for the study of genome-wide functions.

GATA-3 is essential for estrogen response.

GATA-3 binds directly to the SERPIN A3 gene.

The presentation's Take Home Message is:

GATA-3 appears to co-regulate with estrogen receptor.

The audience may forget the exact tools used or which gene is involved, but they stand a good chance of remembering that GATA-3 co-regulates with the estrogen receptor.

By giving both the conclusion points and the subsequent interpretation of their significance, the speaker renders the essential point of the talk more memorable. Here are some other good Take Home Message examples:

Cooling of the brain may decrease its tendency for excitation and seizure.

Generating viruses that express tissue-specific ligands on their outer membranes can allow for highly individualized gene-delivery systems.

The female T-cells are immunized against the Y antigen during pregnancy.

Notice a few things about these examples. They are each scientifically specific, brief, and to the point. They all omit explanatory material that would obviously be defined earlier in the talk. For instance, the Take Home Message, "A2 regulates blood pressure by alternating protein abundance and localization of renal sodium transporters," does not define A2. These Take Home Messages also avoid using vague phrases such as "the role of" and "the effect of," using action verbs that actually describe the role or effect (i.e., decreases, expresses, or immunizes). A precise Take Home Message is both more accurate and more interesting than a wide-ranging one, and thus the audience is more likely to recall it. For example, "Cytosol components directly participate in the membrane fusion between MLV and its host cell," is more memorable than, "Cytosol components are important in membrane fusion." "Poly-boosting is an effective tool for maintaining a strong IFN-8 response during antitumor treatment," is a more accurate Take Home Message than, "Poly-boosting plays a significant role in tumor treatment."

It is common for scientists to give periodic updates to their department without conclusive data. In these cases, the Take Home Message might consist of what has been learned to date, or the presenter's expectations of the current experiments.

As with everything else in a presentation, the Take Home Message should be re-evaluated from time to time. Its wording may be tweaked as the speaker's understanding of her subject evolves, but its essence remains the same. Neither does it change in regard to the audience. A speaker's findings are her findings, whether she addresses high school students or her lab mates. The difference in presenting to these groups will involve degrees of background and definitions (given earlier in the talk), but not the details of the work under discussion.

Incidentally, do not say the term "Take Home Message" in the presentation itself. It and other terms that follow in this book are meant only to facilitate our description of the speech-making process. But regardless of how it is labeled, the Take Home Message is the first step in designing a talk.

Identifying the Main Question

Despite its centrality to a talk, the Take Home Message would be a confusing place to begin. For instance, the statement, "Adult CD4 cells undergo partial polarization under CD3/CD28 costimulation with cytokine priming," clearly lacks context. Even an audience familiar with the subject needs a frame of reference. They need to know what was being studied and what was at stake. To respect an audience's learning process, therefore, consider the following questions: What was the focus of the study? What were the experiments trying to prove?

Identifying this line of inquiry, and boiling it down to a single Main Question, is the second step in the preparation process. The Main Question is the one that will be answered in the talk itself. Like the Take Home Message, it should be brief and specific. Here are some examples:

How does cytosol contribute to membrane fusion?

What are the kinetics of IFN-8 levels during antitumor treatment?

How does brain temperature affect excitation and seizure?

How can we improve the tissue specificity of viral gene-delivery systems?

Which part of the NKCC1 protein is responsible for the formation of the dimer?

These Main Question examples, like good Take Home Messages, substitute action verbs for "the role of" and "the effect of." Also, they are scientifically pertinent, not purely rhetorical. For example, a researcher revised her Main Question, "What are the risk factors for adult stroke?" to the more applicable and scientifically accurate "What factors are at work in the one-third of adult stroke cases that have no clear cause?"

A good Main Question is typically open-ended, beginning with "how," "where," "what," "when" or "why." Complex questions like these are much more engaging than the simple "yes/no" type because, rightly or wrongly, the audience immediately assumes the answer to the latter will be "yes." Occasionally a "yes/no" question is scientifically precise, but it should be used only after careful deliberation. Too often, such questions apply a one-dimensional approach to a multidimensional topic. It is frequently possible to convert a "yes/no" question into an open-ended one simply by substituting a word or two at its start. For instance, "Does HuR protein regulate mRNA?" was rephrased as the more appropriate "How does HuR protein regulate mRNA?" The fact that HuR regulates mRNA was already known; the real question was about its functionality.

Main Questions work best in question form. Following the background of the Introduction, a question stands out as a relevant and topical issue. It also demands a clear and logical response; the speaker cannot help but proceed to answer it. Once she has posed the Main Question, she is more likely to describe each step of the process systematically.

Another way to think of the Main Question is as the query that the Take Home Message answers. In fact, these first two preparation steps act as a good check-and-balance for each other. It is not uncommon to select a Take Home Message, only to realize that it does not accurately match the Main Question of the talk. Should this happen, decide which of the two needs adjusting to integrate the two elements. A Take Home Message that clearly responds to the Main Question reinforces the logic and flow of the entire presentation.

The Main Question is typically a component of a larger study and does not encompass the entire hypothesis. For example, the hypothesis "We want to identify the residues involved in the interaction between the inhibitory receptor of an NK cell and its ligand" boils down to the more manageable Main Question, "Which site is most important in the interaction of Ly49A and H-2D?"

Like the Take Home Message, the Main Question is an information sorter. Because a common speaking mistake is to cram too much information into the talk, both audience and speaker are greatly aided by a clear and defined scope. By being absolutely explicit as to what she will discuss, a speaker reduces the temptation to include related but slightly off-topic material. Which leads to another of the Main Question's benefits: It functions superbly as a focal point for questions after the talk by intrinsically telling the audience, "This (and only this) is the topic under discussion."

A presenter will occasionally identify two Main Questions that deserve equal prominence in a talk. The best tactic, if time permits, is to pose the first question, answer it fully with its corresponding Take Home Message, and then put forward the second question. Posing two questions simultaneously forces speaker and audience to bounce between two sets of data throughout the presentation, a plan that quickly becomes confusing for both parties. Whenever possible, stick to one Main Question; in all other cases, address one at a time.

Once a speaker determines the Main Question, it facilitates the selection of every item of data and every slide in the talk.

CHAPTER 2 CHECKLIST

☐ Pinpoint the Take Home Message.

☐ Identify the Main Question.

3 SELECTING HELPFUL IMAGES

> Science is facts; just as houses are made of stones, so is science made of facts; but a pile of stones is not a house and a collection of facts is not necessarily science.
>
> – Henri Poincaré

In the Hour Glass Format, the Main Question and Take Home Message act as bookends for the Data Section. This section represents the bulk of presentation time and should include all findings, data points and slides.

Because presentation time is of the essence, the speaker must take great care in selecting images. They must be clear, accurate and most representative of the work under discussion. Unfortunately, most speakers are not particularly discriminating at this stage of preparation. Their impulse is to include every piece of data, perhaps on the assumption that a density of information indicates thorough science.

Alas, the opposite is true. Data not tied directly to the Main Question are perplexing for the audience and run the risk of both clouding their understanding and overloading the talk. In other words, too much data make the speaker and the presentation look sloppy and unorganized. The same selectivity required for the Take Home Message and Main Question applies to choosing images.

The Money Slide

We recognized the need for this preparation step after Dr. Robert Massey at the National Institutes of Health relayed a horror story. He drove from Bethesda, Maryland to a meeting in Philadelphia (a trip of about two and a half hours), where he was allowed only two minutes to present, and drove back. As extreme as this example may seem, it spawned a valuable preparation step.

Begin selecting slides by picking out the single most important figure. We call it the Money Slide because it is the most compelling image – the one that would make grant adjudicators reach for their checkbooks. Choosing this illustration is the third major step in preparation.

The Money Slide could be one of several things: the most important finding, one that encompasses all the data or one that indicates expected findings. All other images, schematics, graphs, charts and photographs will in some way relate to or support the Money Slide.

When a speaker isolates the Money Slide from the many other data points the talk contains, he ensures that he will address the most important piece of information, even in the shortest of talks. During presentation, this image also reminds him to give the central finding heightened emphasis. For longer presentations, knowing the Money Slide gives flow and continuity to the entire slide deck.

The sheer importance of the Money Slide can make it tempting to pack as much information onto it as possible. For an example, look at Figure 3.1.

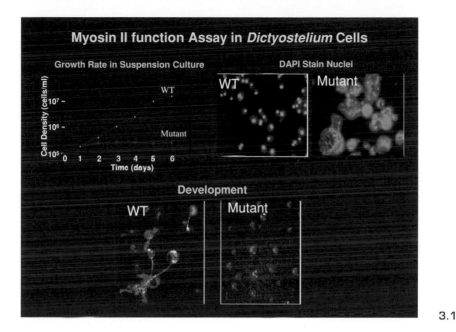

3.1

Although the speaker initially believed this to be a single Money Slide, it is actually three slides in one. By reducing the relative size of each of the three sets of results, the speaker deprives them all of clarity and impact. This large block of data also forces the audience to take in the three images simultaneously.

After further reflection, the speaker selected the second set (DAPI Stain Nuclei) as the Money Slide (Figure 3.2).

This change improves the slide in several ways. Not only are the crucial data now easier to see and understand; they also represent a better use of space. If the Money Slide is truly important, it warrants a full screen. The other two slides in Figure 3.1 would then have more "breathing room" as well.

Regardless of a talk's length, the entire set of slides will lead toward, support or revolve around the Money Slide. Now the obvious question is, "How many slides should that include?"

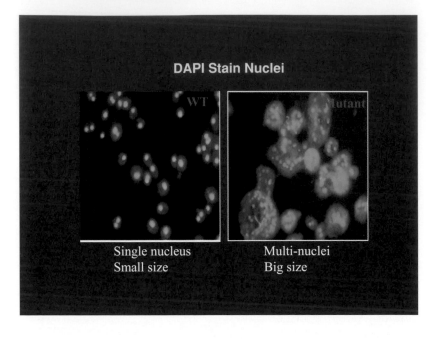

3.2

Supporting Slides

During a recent flight, Scott Morgan was seated next to a pharmaco-logist working furiously on her laptop. She complained that usually she had two hours to present, but this time she had been given only 45 minutes. "It's killing me to cut stuff out," she lamented. Beginning with the Money Slide would have centered the talk and eased her anxiety. And there is another tool for use in selecting supporting images: the "Two Minutes a Slide Rule."

The "Two Minutes a Slide Rule" is a simple formula for estimating how many points can comfortably be covered in a talk, helping to strike a balance between too much and not enough.

This rule works just as it sounds: Take the number of minutes allowed for the talk and divide by two. That should be the maximum number of slides presented, including those in the summary. A 10-minute talk should aim for five slides. There is no cause for concern with six, but a speaker who uses nine or more is simply asking the audience to absorb too much. At some point, he will have to race through the remaining slides, outstripping the audience's comprehension and causing disengagement and confusion.

When approaching the task of choosing the supporting slides, perhaps it is best not to think about images at all. Consider instead the work actually performed in the course of answering the Main Question. Write down each finding and determine which points have a corresponding image to illustrate them. This list then becomes the "plot points" of the talk. Next, apply the "Two Minutes a Slide Rule." If there are still too many slides for the talk's length, refine the list to the points that best represent the experimental process. Unfortunately, due to time constraints, it is often necessary to show only highlights.

Adding the supporting slides is step four in the preparation process. As with the Money Slide, guidelines for clarity and legibility apply to the design of every image.

Good Slide, Bad Slide

All slides should be as easy to describe and to comprehend as the Money Slide, whether the presentation contains two images or a hundred. To help speakers make each one as clear as possible, we have collected samples of images from talks we have attended. These pictures illustrate qualities of both effective and ineffective visual aids. More importantly, they indicate the underlying principles of good visual communication.

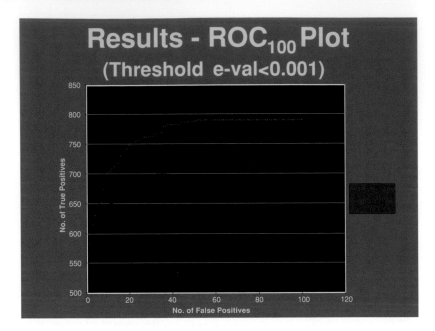

3.3

CONTRAST, FONT SIZE AND "SPIN"

First, no slide should draw attention to its color, or be difficult to read because of it. This example shows the importance of using strong contrast to create effective slides. It is hard to differentiate the dark purple background in Figure 3.3 from the black, dark red and blue on the graph. High contrast between the foreground and background is also the safest way to ensure legibility in a variety of lighting conditions.

Second, notice how much space the main title and subtitle occupy on the image. A title can be helpful as either a label or a reminder of methodology, but it should not require a quarter of the image space. The presenter could give the information in the subtitle verbally, and remove it from the slide altogether. A better choice is pictured in Figure 3.4.

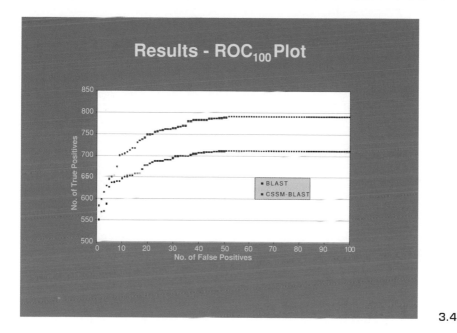

3.4

However, the key findings in neither figure receive their due. The image's critical points include the rapid ascent of true positives measurable by CSSM-BLAST over BLAST, and the persistence of that gap with the increase in the number of false positives. If this graph were to appear in a paper, the reader could linger over the data. But in a talk, the speaker has only one chance to make the graph clear, and so he must help the audience ascertain its most significant feature as quickly as possible. If the slide cannot be remade for practical or political purposes, then at the very least, highlight the critical threshold with a laser pointer as soon as the image appears. Viewers will then be less tempted to devise their own theories as to what part of the slide is most relevant.

Because so much emphasis in scientific talks is placed on visual aids, there is a tendency for speakers to speed through the data without giving them much discussion. They often assume that their results are self-explanatory; in doing so they jeopardize the audience's full comprehension of the talk. These presenters are missing out on a crucial facet of presenting data: not the data itself, but rather the analysis of what they mean. We refer to this analysis as "spin."

An audience attends a presentation not only to see facts and figures, but also to hear the scientist's commentary about them. Without this discussion, the results are relatively meaningless, and listeners are left to guess the significance of the data on their own. When a speaker fails to include spin after every finding, his oral logic quickly becomes hazy. And contrary to popular belief, no slide can or should be expected to explain itself. Therefore, every time a finding is described, explain its significance before moving to the next one. Another way to define spin is as the conclusion point to a given piece of data, the results of which determined the next phase of experimentation. We give examples of how to integrate spin with images in Chapter 6: Delivery.

The linear process of research is an excellent template to apply at every stage in both preparing and presenting a talk. One sentence is all that is needed for adequate spin; it adds very little length to the presentation while dramatically increasing its clarity.

AMOUNT OF DATA AND HIGHLIGHTING

With its high visual contrast, Figure 3.5[1] is an improvement over Figure 3.3, but it has too many numbers. Typically a speaker uses a slide such as this to show (implicitly or explicitly) how thoroughly he performed the work. However, the chances are slim that he will discuss every numerical relationship on the slide. So it is imperative that he "highlight" the crucial relationships – the ones most

---

[1] Pascualvaca, D. M., Fantie, B. D., Papageorgiou, M., & Mirsky, A. F. (1999). *Journal of Autism and Developmental Disorders, 28,* 467–78. With kind permission of Springer Science and Business Media.

The Wisconsin Card Sorting Test

	PDD Children (N=23)	Verbal Matched Controls (N=23)	Performance Matched Controls (N=23)	
Trials to first Category	12.5 (14.7)	16.8 (13.9)	16.3 (13.8)	NS
Failure to maintain set	.4 (6)	1.1 (.9)	.8 (.8)	PDD < C
Number of Categories	2.1 (2.1)	3.9 (1.9)	4.3 (1.9)	PDD < C
Perseverative Errors (%)	48.8 (21.3)	20.4 (14.2)	19.9 (14.1)	PDD < C

3.5

pertinent to the Main Question. For instance, this can be done by enlarging the font size of the most important figures, changing their color or drawing a box around them.

As soon as a slide appears onscreen, a presenter must, in effect, race against the audience's natural response to quickly make sense of the data. One of the benefits of going to a talk is to get information directly from an expert – to ask his help in sifting through mountains of information to get at the pertinent details. An audience assumes that any image an expert presents must be crucial, and in response, they start to interpret the data as soon they appear on the screen. The presenter must honor this reflex not only by showing relevant images, but also by guiding the viewer's attention to the most relevant part of each image. This is another way that he can control the rate and flow of information, ensuring that everyone present is united in the learning process.

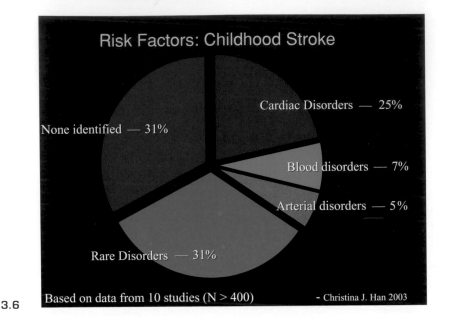

COLOR, CHARTS AND ACKNOWLEDGMENTS

Figure 3.6 has many good qualities. It helps an audience to quickly grasp a series of relationships that would take a lot of time to describe orally. One advantage of cartoons, schematics, bar graphs and pie charts is that they can give a lot of information at a glance.

Notice too that the presenter has given acknowledgment for the source of the data, placing the name in the lower right-hand corner. This is the ideal location for an acknowledgment. There is no need for him to stop the talk and personally thank Dr. Han – unless, of course, she is in attendance. A second option is to place an acknowledgment slide toward the end of the talk, and simply leave it there for a moment without reading the names aloud. In any event, refrain from beginning a talk with acknowledgments of any kind, even of mentors. Doing so reduces the speaker's aura of expertise and begins the presentation on a weak, almost apologetic note.

BUSY SCHEMATICS AND EXPLANATORY TITLES

Figure 3.7 has plenty of good color and simple shapes, but it is incredibly busy. There is a flipside to the "Two Minutes a Slide Rule": An illustration that takes longer than two minutes to describe is probably too complicated. Some information on it should either be removed or divided between two slides. Even if the drawing appears in stages via animation, the overall visual effect obstructs the crucial component. Anything included on a slide must be addressed orally; otherwise it does not belong there.

As it happens, the left side of Figure 3.7 is not relevant to the talk. For all these reasons, the speaker revised the image, as shown in Figure 3.8.

The compounds extraneous to the Main Question have been removed, so neither the speaker nor the audience is distracted

3.7

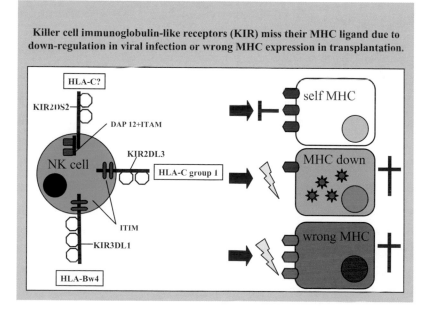

Killer cell immunoglobulin-like receptors (KIR) miss their MHC ligand due to down-regulation in viral infection or wrong MHC expression in transplantation.

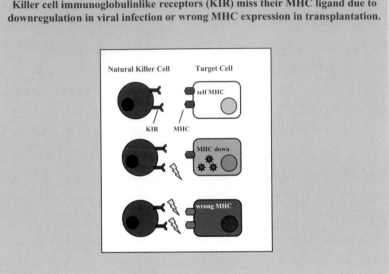

Killer cell immunoglobulinlike receptors (KIR) miss their MHC ligand due to downregulation in viral infection or wrong MHC expression in transplantation.

3.8

by them. In its relative simplicity and focus, Figure 3.8 is much improved over Figure 3.7.

But both of them still contain a problematic element: the explanatory title. Titles like this one, which essentially consist of the spin inscribed on the slide, are common. They may ease a presenter's fear of forgetting something important, but the drawback is that the slide's conclusion is visible to all before he has a chance to say it. There is almost always more to describe before the presenter reveals the ultimate point of the data, so printing the spin on the slide allows the audience to get ahead of him. Far from a dynamic teaching tool, the image then becomes "stale," while the audience waits for the speaker to catch up.

This method of title design also fails to reflect the actual chronology of the work: When experimentation began, the speaker did not know the outcome. Receiving the information in reverse order impedes an audience's ability to assimilate it. They learn best by following the same scientific order that the speaker followed, albeit in compressed time.

Besides, the schematics alone do not prove that the KIR "miss their MHC ligand due to down-regulation in viral infection or wrong MHC expression in transplantation," as stated in the titles of Figures 3.7 and 3.8. A schematic's primary value is to help the audience visualize the relationship between its depicted elements; *explaining* that relationship is the speaker's job.

LEGENDS AND GRAPHS

Figure 3.9[2] is an all too common example of copying an image from a paper for use in a talk. For many viewers, it is confusing to connect the legend with the corresponding lines on the graph; it is no easier to do when the image is projected on a large screen. As in Figures 3.7 and 3.8, the spin is also printed as the title.

The most noticeable improvement of Figure 3.10[2] is the use of color. Red was added to Tdp1 both on the graph and in the legend. This simple change enables the differentiating factor to stand out more clearly. However, the light blue of Top1 will vanish when shown on a large screen. In general, avoid pastels on slides (unless against a very dark background); they bleach out when projected. Also, do not use red/green as a compare-and-contrast tool on the same slide. Those who are colorblind will not be able to see the difference.

The legend in Figure 3.10 now matches the lines on the graph in terms of north/south orientation. For maximum clarity, a legend should always correspond to the lines at the point where they terminate along the x axis.

---

[2] Liu, C., Pouliot, J. J. and Nash, H. A. *The Role of Tdp1 from Budding Yeast in the Repair of DNA Damage*. DNA Repair (Amst.) 2004 Jun 3;3 (6): 593-601. Printed with kind permission from Elsevier.

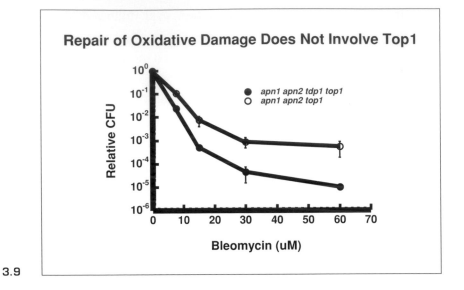

Repair of Oxidative Damage Does Not Involve Top1

3.9

3.10

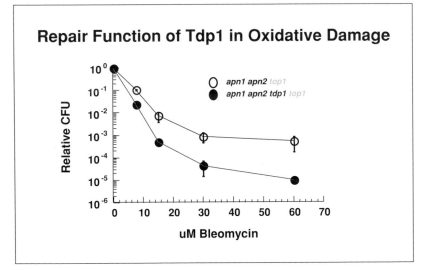

Repair Function of Tdp1 in Oxidative Damage

Another improvement is that the title no longer functions as spin. Instead, it merely labels the data without giving away the conclusion prematurely.

CONCLUSION POINTS AND TEXT SLIDES

Too often, the conclusion slide appears to consist of new information because the speaker presents it as new information. Conclusion points should be no more than a reminder of the spin for each previously discussed data point. In addition, the complex sentence structure used in Figure 3.11 makes following these points more difficult for the audience.

This example also presents a more fundamental problem. Slides that consist solely of text promote a disjunction between the speaker and viewer. A speaker may think the concepts are clear because they are written out for all to see and that there is no conceivable way of misconstruing them. But in practice, a text-only slide wields many stumbling blocks that actually impede clarity.

3.11

Conclusions:

- FCS provides sensitive technique to detect changes in local structure of PVA solutions and gels due to varying polymer concentration and cross-link density

- FCS measurements indicate
  - TAMRA molecules diffuse more slowly in gels than in the corresponding solutions
  - diffusion time in solutions and gels increases linearly with concentration of polymer
  - At fixed polymer concentration, diffusion time increases with cross-link density

- Found a linear relationship between τ_d (dynamic) and G (static)
  (for range of concentration and cross-link density studied)

Consider the options for a speaker who uses a text-heavy slide. One is for him to read the text aloud, which requires him to turn his back to the audience. Because the lifeblood of a presentation is contact between speaker and audience, this is a dangerous habit to develop. Also, it is highly unlikely that every member of the audience will read at the same pace as the presenter. Some members of the audience may be on conclusion point number four while the speaker is still discussing point number two. Even in the best scenarios, the audience will see lots of text on the screen and immediately look to the speaker for assistance; in a public speaking setting, we would all rather listen than read. Another problem is that the presenter cannot easily deviate from the scripted words. If he makes even minor adjustments to the text onscreen, the audience hears one explanation while reading another, creating at least momentary confusion. Besides, as the speaker's analysis of data evolves over time, the wording used to describe it evolves as well. Better not to commit to a precise set of words that will undoubtedly change.

We occasionally hear the comment that putting text on the screen addresses the needs of those who best learn visually. However, we are talking about the problem of dual input, not learning preferences. To draw an analogy outside of science, it is extremely difficult to listen to a CNN anchorperson while reading the running text (or "crawl") at the bottom of the screen, even if the subject in both cases is the same. Comprehending different information streams simultaneously is virtually impossible.

Years of observation have shown the authors that text slides are primarily used for the presenter's benefit rather than to facilitate the audience's understanding. In other words, the slides function as cue cards.

As a first step away from using text-heavy slides, try using note cards with only key words and/or phrases written on them instead.

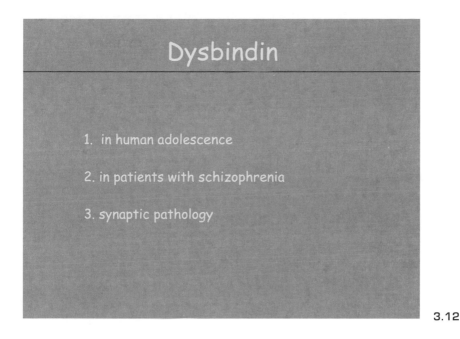

3.12

Perhaps in an ideal presentation, the speaker would be so comfortable with the material that he would need no notes whatsoever. But until that point, note cards are an excellent tool to increase speaker/audience interaction. They are certainly preferable to the other common options: reading from the screen, reading from full sheets of paper, or trying to commit the entire piece to memory. By periodically glancing at the cards to keep himself on track, a speaker can deliver the talk spontaneously while keeping most of his eye contact and attention where it belongs: on the audience.

For the many reasons listed above, always avoid putting full sentences on slides. The effect of text-only slides on comprehension levels is sufficient reason to approach them with extreme caution.

For those who appreciate the dangers of text slides yet do not wish to part with them entirely, an alternate method of presenting them can be useful. An example is in Figure 3.12.

The brevity of the text in this example, as compared with the full sentences in Figure 3.11, reduces the chances of splitting the audience's focus. It would be even more beneficial to reveal the bullet points one at a time – a useful tool of PowerPoint. The speaker can thereby hold the audience's full attention, and elaborate on each item.

Incidentally, beware of using too much animation and fancy visual effects. They only serve to distract the audience from the material. If a speaker wants certain information to appear later, as in the previous example, then a simple and quick fade-in/fade-out is the best transition. At no point should the audience become aware of a software program's clever tricks.

Clearly, there are several important criteria to apply in selecting and creating the content of visual aids. An image's appearance is as important as its content, and carries equal weight in determining a presentation's success. But it bears remembering that an audience attends a talk primarily to hear a description of the research process and the speaker's interpretation of its meaning. Good slide design should always aim first to aid audience comprehension and absorption of this material.

CHAPTER 3 CHECKLIST

- [ ] Select the Money Slide.
- [ ] Estimate the total slide count.
- [ ] Choose any supporting slides.
- [ ] Verify that there are no full sentences on any slide.

4 BEGINNING AND ENDING THE PRESENTATION

The purpose of models is not to fit the data but to sharpen the questions.

– Samuel Karlin

As nerve-racking as it can be to give a talk, the first few minutes pose the biggest hurdle for a presenter. When the beginning of the talk does not go well, the remainder, not to mention the question and answer period, can seem like an uphill battle. There is no substitute, then, for getting a presentation off to a good start.

If engaging the audience's full attention is a speaker's most important goal, then it is never too early to begin. Some speaking coaches suggest giving the audience a minute or two to "settle in" during opening remarks. A better plan is to begin the talk so strongly that the audience is immediately focused and engaged. The opening sentences of a presentation not only establish its tone, but also provide necessary background for all that will follow. They are too important to treat casually.

This stage of the preparation process is often the most difficult and time-consuming. And to make things more complicated, the beginning of the talk changes with every new audience. Finding the right "hook" can be a troublesome task, but there are practical tactics with which to engage the audience.

Common Ground

An audience may be intrigued by many things. They might be captivated by a speaker's enthusiasm or a mutual interest. But a talk should be more than merely interesting or entertaining. Audiences are most engaged when the speaker tells them how the information ahead will affect their work. A professional application, not merely interest or curiosity, engages attentiveness better than any other device and elevates a talk from "interesting" to "vital." The best way to achieve this immediate connection is to address the work that the speaker and the audience have in common. This work might be called the common denominator, collective goal or Common Ground. It is the fifth element a presenter prepares.

Addressing the shared work via a Common Ground statement serves many purposes. First, it acknowledges the larger issue to which each member of the audience is also contributing. In fact, it can help to think of Common Ground as a brief description of "us" (speaker and audience) versus "the problem." It connects everyone in the room by addressing broader scientific concerns than those of the Main Question.

It may be tempting to start the presentation with definitions of key players (genes, proteins, methods) or with statistics. As a beginning statement, however, definitions or alarming numbers are dry and far too common. They make for a generalized and bland opening. Common Ground is a much more powerful choice because it immediately concentrates on current topics and dilemmas in the field, while respecting the audience's knowledge base.

From the attendees' point of view, the value of the speaker's Main Question is how it contributes to a greater understanding of their own work. Common Ground jump-starts a talk by immediately addressing what interests the attendees the most. It is then the speaker's responsibility to draw an explicit connection between this collective work (Common Ground) and her Main Question. In fact, that is the most important function of the Introduction.

It is not uncommon for a speaker to present before an audience about which she knows very little. She might assume that because Common Ground is not obvious, it must not exist. But the mere act of being asked to present indicates that someone else has identified such a link, although it may take some research to unravel the connection. If need be, ask the lab chief, principal investigator, department head or conference facilitator for insight into the matter: "What will this audience expect to gain from my talk? What issues do we have in common? Why should they care about my topic?"

The Place to Start

To establish Common Ground with any audience, first imagine speaking before a small group of peers. If the opening statements of the talk are to engage one's colleagues, who know a great deal about the field under discussion, those statements must be direct, specific and scientifically relevant. Finding Common Ground among peers is the most difficult and therefore the most helpful step for finding Common Ground with a broader audience.

As an initial step toward identifying these concerns, consider the following speculative questions:

What is the mystery or collective "puzzle" faced by this particular group?

Because no one in the audience is working on this particular Main Question, why should they listen?

What is generally understood about this area of research, and what is still unclear?

What are the current "hot topics" being studied by this group of peers?

Here are some Common Ground statements from speakers who were addressing their colleagues at the lab or branch level:

> Successful cloning by nuclear transplantation into eggs was reported in frogs and several mammalian species. However, we do not know how the transplanted nuclei are remodeled so that the reconstituted eggs can develop normally.

For this statement to be effective as Common Ground, the speaker must have first verified that everyone in the audience is working on the problems of nuclear transplantation. By posing the current dilemmas, the speaker both engages the audience and prepares them for the more specific Main Question to follow.

> In patients with AIDS, systemic therapy slows the progression of Uveitis moderately, but it is associated with toxic effects, inconvenience and high financial cost.

> The premise that publicly supported research results in inventions and discoveries marketed by private industry, ultimately returning benefit to the public, has long been accepted as a matter of public policy. But in fact, the premise has never been quantitatively tested.

The second example establishes a presumption under which audience and speaker had previously been operating. This is also a way to formulate Common Ground.

Yet another way is to state as succinctly as possible what is known and unknown in the field. Addressing current complications says, in effect, "Here is where we are collectively ignorant," as in the following instance:

We now have clear evidence of antiidiotype immune responses in patients with follicular lymphoma, following vaccination with our idiotype vaccine. Despite this, we continue to see some cross reactive antiidiotype immune responses in our in vitro assays. How can we find a more specific immunological target to resolve these cross-reactive immune responses?

Always make sure that everyone in the audience is not just aware of the larger problem, but is actually working on it on a daily basis. For example, here are three versions of a Common Ground statement from the same talk as it might be delivered to three audiences: the lab (or branch), department or a professional meeting.

Lab audience: "I am trying to find proteins that interact with BIG 1 using the yeast two-hybrid system."

Departmental audience: "My lab is particularly interested in which proteins regulate vesicular movements inside the cell."

Professional-meeting audience: "Our department is trying to elucidate how cell vesicular trafficking is regulated."

Common Ground can also be approached by working backward from the more focused, immediate subject of the Main Question to the larger issue of Common Ground. A presenter might ask himself, "What separates my work (Main Question) from the work of my peers (Common Ground)?"

Not only does Common Ground immediately engage the audience, but it also acts as a good gauge in determining the proper amount of introduction to give. In the process of defining the work of the audience, a speaker also defines their level of knowledge, hence reducing the amount of background and the number of definitions needed in the Introduction.

Conversely, if listeners are not intimately familiar with the topic, Common Ground will orient them to the larger context – get them "up to speed" – before the speaker moves into the details. Well-defined Common Ground demonstrates his respect for the audience's time and experience.

Following the Take Home Message, Main Question, Money Slide and Supporting Slides, Common Ground is the next component of the presentation to prepare. Examine how a Common Ground statement is aligned with the Main Question and Take Home Message from the same presentation.

> **Common Ground:** B-cells have been observed to have conflicting dysfunctions in the background of HIV infection.
>
> **Main Question:** How does T helper-cell infection contribute to B-cell dysfunction?
>
> **Take Home Message:** Our research suggests that B-cells show higher dysfunction in the background of high viral load than of low viral load.

Common Ground is appropriate because the speaker has determined that all attendees work on B-cell dysfunction. While the Main Question's subject of T helper-cells will not in itself solve the larger issue of B-cell dysfunction, it may help advance knowledge toward that long-term goal.

The Complete Introduction

As noted in Chapter 1, the Introduction starts with Common Ground and ends with the Main Question. In the space between the two, the speaker should cover previous studies, background information, and any recurring terms that will be discussed in the presentation. One speaker began her talk this way:

> Much progress has been made in recognizing the physiological and mental consequences of ethanol exposure in the developing brain.

However, the specific players, the order and the area of activation have yet to be associated into organized pathways. Increased amounts of apoptosis are one of the prevalent features in Fetal Alcohol Syndrome. As a result, it has become important to know how caspases are involved in ethanol-induced apoptosis. Or more specifically, how does Caspase 3 trigger apoptosis of three-day in vitro cerebral granular cells when exposed to ethanol?

This example constitutes practically an entire Introduction. A few elements are missing, such as an explanation of why Caspase 3 is a logical candidate for study. A good Introduction explains the major decisions that led to the Main Question.

Use the following worksheets to help trace those decisions. The first worksheet, Figure 4.1 (enlarged version of this figure can be found in Appendix 1), is for use in preparing the Introduction of a talk to one's immediate peers. The triangle shape of the worksheet reminds the speaker that the Introduction starts broadly and then narrows in scope as the subject tapers toward the Main

What is the overall aim of the lab or branch? 4.1

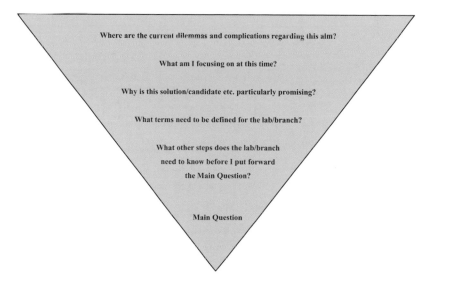

Question. While the speaker would not state the answer to the top-most question aloud, because it is common knowledge, the question is nonetheless useful in laying the groundwork for those that follow. On the other hand, answers to the questions inside the triangle would actually be given during the presentation. If any answer seems obvious, then either it is not specific enough, or perhaps the question does not apply.

For more examples of full Introductions, see Appendix 1.

When giving the same talk for a broader group, adapt Common Ground to the work of the new audience. The next two worksheets [Figures 4.2 and 4.3 (enlarged versions of these figures can be found in Appendix 1)] correspond to two increasingly broader audiences. This format could be expanded further to engage the broadest audience of all, the general public.

Giving such detailed thought to the Introduction is relatively time consuming. But in the long run, the effort actually saves the speaker

4.2

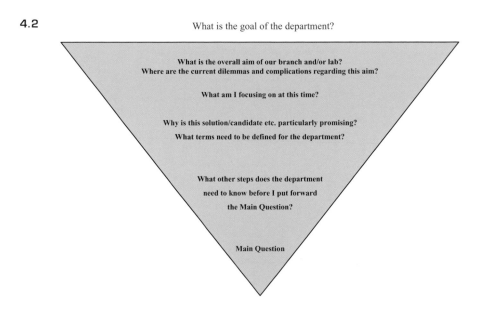

What is the goal of the department?

What is the overall aim of our branch and/or lab?
Where are the current dilemmas and complications regarding this aim?

What am I focusing on at this time?

Why is this solution/candidate etc. particularly promising?
What terms need to be defined for the department?

What other steps does the department
need to know before I put forward
the Main Question?

Main Question

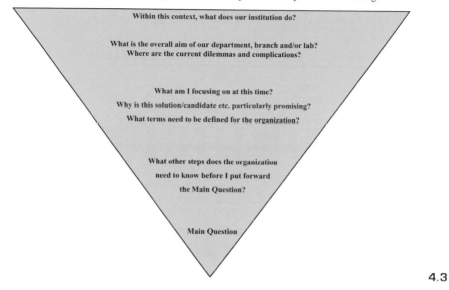

What is the purpose of the organization or the objective of the professional meeting?

Within this context, what does our institution do?

What is the overall aim of our department, branch and/or lab?
Where are the current dilemmas and complications?

What am I focusing on at this time?
Why is this solution/candidate etc. particularly promising?
What terms need to be defined for the organization?

What other steps does the organization
need to know before I put forward
the Main Question?

Main Question

4.3

a lot of work by defining in advance the amount of background information a given audience will require.

Regardless of the audience, however, the rest of the presentation after the Main Question will change very little. An audience is willing to delve into even the most detailed experimentation, as long as the Introduction has accurately addressed their particular work.

Danger: Introductory Slides Ahead

Another strategy for crafting a good Introduction is to resist presenting any visual aids until after the Main Question. An audience uses the Introduction to grow accustomed to a speaker's vocal patterns, mannerisms, and body language. At the same time, they are concentrating on the concepts, relevance, rationale, oral logic, key terms, purpose and goals. Presenting a slide in these early stages can

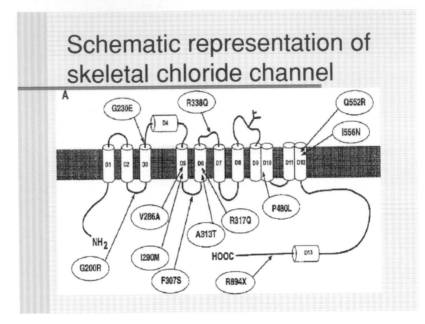

4.4

only interfere with their absorption process. They are being asked to grasp the particulars of the work without knowing why.

For example, schematics such as the one in Figure 4.4 only serve to bewilder viewers unless the speaker poses the Main Question first. Until the audience knows the scientific context for the image, it comes across as random information. However, if Figure 4.4 is presented after the Main Question, "Among the mutations in the CLCN 1 gene, what is the function of the variant G230E in domain 3?", then the drawing becomes a tool for visualizing the relevant components.

The Introduction should highlight the course of thought that led to the Main Question. Following this conceptual discussion, pictures make better sense, and the audience and presenter remain in step with each other. For this reason, we often refer to the Introduction as "Section Why." Because it provides the rationale for asking the Main Question, nothing should distract the audience from hearing it fully.

Occasionally, a speaker is tempted to use a muddled title slide such as the one in Figure 4.5.

This speaker may think that a visual allusion to the many aspects of Kaposi's Sarcoma will help the audience appreciate the importance of the disease. However, she has unintentionally generated a lot of visual static that sends conflicting messages to the audience. The clutter of pictures provokes such questions as, "Is the speaker going to discuss the symptomatic responses? New methods of tracking microphage infection? Or perhaps the polarization of AZT crystals?" The slide sends the audience in a variety of potential directions before the presentation has even begun.

4.5

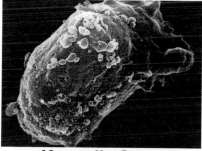
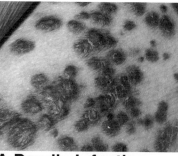

Kaposi's Sarcoma: A Deadly Infection

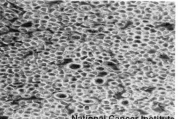

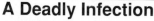
National Cancer Institute

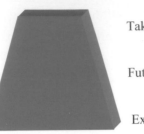

Take Home Message

Future Plans

Exit Line

4.6

Wrapping It Up

After working hard on the Introduction and the Data Section, speakers often neglect to plan the final portion of the talk. And so an otherwise effective presentation ends weakly. Like a good story, a good talk should have a strong, clear ending.

The Resolution Section (Figure 4.6) wraps up the presentation with any ancillary information that the speaker may want to include: design limitations, inherent biases or a brief synopsis. But the main function of the Resolution Section is to discuss prospective projects. Closing with future studies gives the audience a sense of how the speaker's work will continue, and how that work might affect their own.

The Resolution Section concludes with the Exit Line, which is the sixth element to prepare. Consisting of only a sentence or two, the Exit Line concludes the talk proper before the speaker proceeds to questions. Here are some good examples:

> Our goal over the next several months is to test this single-chain protein in assays to assess human response. We will also insert this gene into the patients' own B-cells, to test whether they are either tumor-specific or idiotype-specific CTL.

> In aggregate, puromycin attenuates the activities of store-operated calcium channels. Our next studies will determine whether puromycin acts directly or indirectly on these channels.

Compared to the other signposts of a talk, the Exit Line is relatively malleable and may even change mid-thought. Nonetheless, preparing it assures the speaker that she has planned the talk from beginning to end, and that she will not leave the final thoughts to improvisation.

CHAPTER 4 CHECKLIST

☐ Define Common Ground.

☐ Plot an outline of the Introduction with the appropriate worksheet.

☐ Avoid using visual aids in the Introduction.

☐ Specify future directions.

☐ Prepare a strong Exit Line.

5 TITLING THE TALK

The problem of creating something which is new, but which is consistent with everything which has been seen before, is one of extreme difficulty.

– Richard P. Feynman

The seventh and final step in preparation is to decide on the title. And titling a talk requires a different approach from titling a paper.

A title's function in a paper is twofold. The first is to identify the subject and address the major research finding. The second is to act as a reliable "magnet" for internet or other searches (such as Medline). The greater the number of pertinent words in the title, the more matches the search will produce. Consequently, a writer might be rewarded by making the title both lengthy and nearly exhaustive in its description of the paper's content.

When it comes to a presentation title, however, length and exhaustiveness are liabilities. This is mainly due to the fact that the "search mechanisms" associated with a talk are quite different. Presentation titles are most likely posted in a conference schedule, calendar, dedicated flyer or email. Under these circumstances, attendees assume that the title represents only the highlights of the subject, not its every facet. The title, therefore, should reflect only those highlights. The audience expects to hear the specifics in the talk itself.

A title for a talk also needs to attract attention, for the obvious reason that it usually competes with other presentations. In a conference setting, for example, attendees must choose between several talks in a given time period, using titles as their principal guide. Or, if the presentation is a stand-alone event, they must weigh their attendance against other obligations. A title has only a few seconds to capture audience interest either way. So an effective title must not only be scientifically accurate, it must also be appealing.

Identifying both the Main Question and Common Ground of the talk is the best possible rehearsal for crafting a precise and engaging title. Common Ground acknowledges the bigger picture; the Main Question supplies the focus. When a speaker waits until step seven to create the title, the result is more likely to reflect these structural elements.

The following example is typical of many presentation titles:

The Design and Application of Tagging SNPs in Neuronally Expressed Voltage-Gated Sodium Channel Genes to a Cohort of Caucasian Epilepsy Patients[1]

The main point of this title becomes clear only after repeated readings. Because of its length and meandering style, the thread of its meaning is momentarily lost. In the author's attempt to be specific, he has added too many details. The phrase "to a cohort of Caucasian epilepsy patients" is meant to qualify the study's subjects, but it gives the impression that the presentation will only be relevant to those studying epilepsy among Caucasian patients. Secondly, the more engaging element of the title – tagging SNPs – is diffused by its length.

---

[1] Gianpiero L. Cavalleri, Institute of Genome Sciences and Policy, Duke University.

"Epilepsy" is important for the title, but the fact that the patients are Caucasian is not. "The design and application" is implicit and so can be removed, as could "patients." "Neuronally expressed" might be too detailed; "to a cohort" may be obvious. An improved title may look more like this:

Tagging SNPs: Voltage-Gated Sodium Channel Genes in Epilepsy

The first way to make a title engaging, then, is to be brief. Aim for no more than eight to 10 words. Attendees looking over a competitive listing of events (often in the few minutes between presentations) may avoid a talk with an overly detailed title in favor of a talk with a briefer one.

To begin trimming extraneous words from the title, look first for what is essential to convey the core subject of the presentation. For example:

Delay of Epiphyseal Fusion: An Experimental Approach for Increasing the Height of Extremely Short Children[2]

The thrust of this talk would seem to be the "delay of epiphyseal fusion," which is also the most explicit term in the title. Probably the phrase "increasing the height of children" also belongs, since it serves an explanatory function. As for the remainder, the speaker should reconsider whether "extremely short" is necessary. If this is a precise clinical term, then it may belong; if not, then it probably does not. In any case, the phrase "an experimental approach for" is implicit and can be omitted. A possible reworking of the title may look like this:

Delay of Epiphyseal Fusion: Increasing the Height of Short Children

---

[2] Yanovski, J. A., Grand Rounds, National Institutes of Health, August 1997.

On the other hand, it is possible for a title to be too short. For instance:

Schizophrenia in the Age of Molecular Science[3]

In an effort to be brief, this speaker has come up with a broad, generic title, better suited for a week's seminar than for a single presentation. Its vagueness is unlikely to attract the appropriate attendees; precision is always favorable to generalities. The challenge is not simply to be brief, but to balance brevity with clarity.

By clarity, however, we do not mean to imply that a title should consist of the Take Home Message. In fact, another way to shorten a title and make it more engaging is to ensure that it does *not* include the Take Home Message. Look at the following example:

Activation of Hippocampal Formation Reflects Success in Both Encoding and Cued Recall of Paired Associates[4]

The verb "reflects" signals a giveaway of the presentation's overall message. Titling with the Take Home Message places the audience well ahead of the speaker. And if he wants the audience to follow his scientific logic, then the oral logic of the talk must follow the same sequence. This is the same reasoning for placing the Take Home Message late in the presentation. Hence, the Take Home Message is best left out of the title. The title of a paper may often preview the Take Home Message, but the most effective talk titles do not.

An alternate title for the same presentation might be:

[3] Pickar, D., Grand Rounds, National Institutes of Health, August 1997.
[4] Meltzer, J. A., Constable, R. T., *Neuroimage* (USA), Jan 15 2005, 24(2) 384–97.

Applying Hippocampal Formation to Encoding and Cued Recall

Here is another example of a title containing the Take Home
Message:

Event-Related fMRI Reveals Two Human Cortical Mechanisms during a Working Memory Task[5]

It was changed to:

Déjà Vu in Working Memory: Event-Related fMRI

Not only is the second title catchier, it is also much better without "reveals," which divulges the main point. As with any other
text slide, it is best to avoid full sentences (i.e., verbs) when titling
a talk.

The previous title does something else effectively. Its opening
phrase, "Déjà vu in Working Memory," alludes to the presentation's
Common Ground, while the subtitle hints at the Main Question. In
other words, the title starts with the more general issue before proceeding to the more specific topic. The heading starts broadly and
then narrows, much as the Introduction does as a whole. With this
in mind, the earlier Epiphyseal Fusion title can be further improved
by reversing its first and second phrases:

Increasing the Height of Short Children: The Delay of Epiphyseal Fusion

"Increasing the Height of Short Children" alludes to the broader
Common Ground, while "Delay of Epiphyseal Fusion" indicates the
more refined focus of the Main Question.

---

[5] Jiang, Y., Haxby, J. V., Martin, A., Maisog, J. M., Ungerleider, L. G. and Parasuraman,
R., Oral Abstract, Fourth International Conference on Functional Mapping of the
Human Brain, 1998.

CHAPTER 5 CHECKLIST

☐ Craft a precise title for the subject.

☐ Edit the title for brevity – short but not vague.

☐ Do not include the Take Home Message in the title.

☐ Place the broader information first, followed by the more specific.

At a Glance

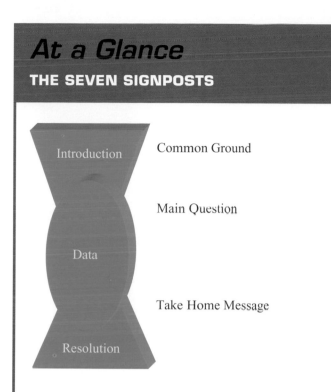

Common Ground

Main Question

Take Home Message

PREPARATION ORDER

1   Take Home Message

2   Main Question

3   Money Slide

4   Supporting Slides

5   Common Ground

6   Exit Line

7   Title

For a full transcript of a 10-minute presentation incorporating all these signposts, go to www.premierepublicspeaking.com.

6 DELIVERY

Science is not the dispassionate analysis of impartial data. It is the human, and thus passionate, exercise of skill and sense on such data.

– Philip Hilts

As we have seen, presenting a talk well actually begins with the first step of preparation. The confidence that results from both having a clear message, and knowing how to guide listeners to it, is a major step toward success.

The many preparation steps involved in creating a presentation come together in the act of delivery. In this chapter, we look at some techniques that help a speaker confront the challenges of presenting, beginning with a nearly universal one: nervousness.

Stage Fright

The most common fear about giving a presentation revolves around fear itself. Many people wonder how the best public speakers overcome this fear – hoping, perhaps, that there is a magic pill to cure it. The unavoidable fact is that, when it comes to public speaking, nervousness never goes away entirely. However, as the Latin proverb says, "Our fears always outnumber our dangers."

As of this writing, the authors have performed and presented for a combined total of nearly 50 years. Each has been told that he must be one of those "natural speakers." Yet both still feel butterflies in the stomach before taking the podium. That is because standing in front of others always involves a degree of risk: that of making a mistake, of being judged, of a technological failure, and so forth. But effective speakers have discovered that this risk does not have to be debilitating.

In fact, a speaker needs some degree of nervousness to give the best presentation possible. However, this heightened sensation is better thought of as excitement rather than as fear. Very few people give talks for eight hours a day, so the novelty of presenting can (and should) lend a little extra energy to the performance. Every presentation needs that spark; without excitement, a talk would be dull to give and boring to attend. Any effort to become "totally relaxed" before presenting is not only pointless but also potentially damaging to the act of communication. In the context of public speaking, relaxation is a myth. A better plan is to redirect anxious energy, so that it becomes productive – or as another adage goes, "The goal is not to get rid of the butterflies, but to get them to fly in formation."

One accomplishes this goal not by denying nervousness, but by allowing it its rightful place. Before giving a talk, each author usually murmurs to himself something like, "I may be nervous, but I have an important message to give, and fear is not going to prevent me from sharing it." Acknowledging an uncomfortable feeling relaxes its grip on the mind, so less energy is spent trying to bottle it up. It is easier to focus on the task at hand when one acknowledges anxiety without dwelling on it.

It can also be helpful to remember that the content of the talk, and not the speaker, is the true focal point for the audience. The speaker is no more (and no less) than a conduit for the subject matter. That is another reason that good, thorough preparation is such a valuable asset: The more a speaker is assured of her primary message, the more attention she can train on clear delivery, instead of on how the audience perceives her personally. Effective delivery results when the content stays front and center in her mind.

Knowing what a speaker undergoes physiologically can be a further step toward coping with stage fright. A stressful episode consists of three distinct stages. The first, the "alarm stage," begins with the initial perception of threat. For a speaker, that might be when she receives a request to present, at the moment she is introduced to the audience, or even when she imagines talking to an unknown audience at an undetermined date. In the alarm stage, a speaker typically experiences increased levels of adrenaline, sweating and rapid breathing among other symptoms.

The second phase of stress, the "resistance stage," takes place when she devotes attention to something other than the perceived danger. The body reduces its release of adrenaline and other physical responses that had intensified the stressful sensation. The presenter is left alert rather than agitated. In speaking situations, this stage might occur after the speaker says the first few sentences. A well thought-out opening gets her through the early moments of anxiety; a focused talk helps focus the speaker's emotions.

The third stage, the "phase of exhaustion," occurs after the threat has passed entirely (at some point following the end of the talk) and true relaxation is again possible.

Even in the resistance stage, a nagging problem for many presenters is the "internal critic." This is the inner voice that pipes up during a talk to say such things as, "The audience is bored," "You've lost them," or, "You really don't know what you're talking about." The internal critic can pose a serious distraction by sapping a speaker's confidence. But it is also a voice that, viewed differently, can be of genuine assistance.

The internal critic actually wants us to improve as speakers and therefore should not be silenced. But it needs a productive job. Shortly before presenting, ask the critic to take copious notes on all aspects of the presentation, but not to interrupt during the talk. Afterward, check in with the critic and listen to its comments. They are almost always on-target and surprisingly gentle. Make sure to listen thoroughly, however, or the critic is likely to interrupt during the next talk. Treated respectfully, the internal critic frees the speaker to give the best presentation possible and provides useful feedback afterward, fueling her self-confidence.

Teaching vs. Lecturing

When it comes to delivery, speakers are often concerned with such matters as their gestures, voice, posture, movement and so on. Whereas these matters merit some attention, a more crucial aspect of delivery is tone. A presenter's tone is the attitude informing a talk that, in addition to clarity of content, will determine how well an audience understands the presentation. The "us versus the problem" approach proposed in the Common Ground section of Chapter 4 conveys a speaker's respect by giving the audience just the right amount of background. When she incorporates a teaching tone, an audience recognizes that the objective is to assist them, and they reciprocate that regard. Thought of this way, the talk becomes a means of educating the audience. A good speaker is a good teacher.

Perhaps this description of a teaching tone sounds a bit abstract, but it has demonstrable positive effects. When a presenter wants an audience to learn and absorb, she usually speaks more slowly and states the key terms clearly and audibly.

A good teacher is also cognizant of the clock. She knows how much information she can comfortably relate in the scheduled time frame. Time management also prevents one of the cardinal sins of public speaking: exceeding the allotted time. Besides showing reverence for the audience, a speaker who respects the time constraints appears to be a more disciplined scientist. In fact, we strongly suggest that all speakers end their presentations early.

Lastly, the elements of the Hour Glass Format further support the task of teaching. The Main Question, in effect, provides the syllabus, defining the extent of information to be covered. The "Two Minutes a Slide Rule" provides the speaker with enough time to adequately describe each finding. Interpreting each data point emphasizes the research process. The Take Home Message assures a central theme. The use of all these structural components helps a speaker present in such a way that teaching is the natural result.

The alternative to teaching is lecturing. When lecturing, a speaker covers too much information too quickly, uses little eye contact and conveys an apparent disregard for the thoughts and ideas behind the data. A lecturing tone suggests that a speaker is indifferent to how well the audience is absorbing the material. In short, it undermines the entire purpose of a presentation.

Three Steps for Presenting Data

There is an indispensable teaching tool for sharpening the impact of the Data Section. It is a methodical, three-step process we recommend for presenting visual images. As mentioned, there is only one chance to make an image understood, and the speaker must help the audience ascertain the most significant feature of each image as quickly as possible. The best way to accomplish this task is to begin describing the data even before the slide is on the screen.

The first step, then, is to set up or "preview" the upcoming image. Preview consists of no more than a sentence or two in which the presenter introduces what the audience is about to see. A simple statement such as, "I've plotted that on a graph," or, "Here are the results after running PCR," shows that the speaker, and not PowerPoint, is in control of the presentation. A good rule of thumb is that when she is ready for the audience to see a given set of results, then the amount of preface has been sufficient.

Conversely, when a speaker does not preview her images, it appears to observers as though she needs the slides to speak about them; as a consequence, her expertise is diminished in the viewers' eyes. We say "appears," because obviously the speaker is no less knowledgeable about the subject whether she previews the slides or not. Nonetheless, if the slides function as cue cards, they diminish a scientist's apparent proficiency.

The second step in presenting data is to "highlight" the image, a technique mentioned in Chapter 3. The speaker brings the picture up on the screen and discusses the important parts. As obvious as this step may seem, it should not be treated lightly. As soon as they see the image, an audience immediately looks for any visual indication of results, regardless of what the speaker may have to say first. Without proper highlighting, they will form their own opinions. This reaction is as likely when the audience consists of one's peers, who may have some knowledge of the subject. Highlighting assures that the audience and the speaker are examining the same visual material at the same time.

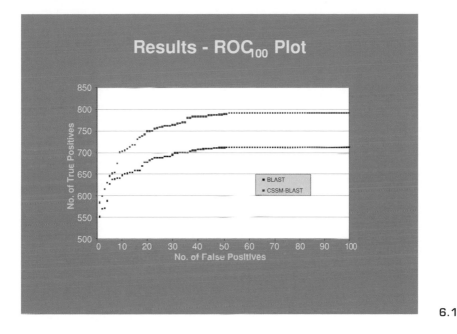

6.1

The third step in presenting data is to give "spin" to the image. The speaker explains the significance of the data she just highlighted. Spin is a brief yet essential step in articulating how each finding leads to the next.

Here is an example of the three-step process. The preview for Figure 6.1 might be: "The next graph shows the results of an ROC Plot comparing BLAST and CSSM-BLAST." Then, the speaker would bring up Figure 6.1 on the screen.

Highlight: "First, notice the rapid increase of true positives measurable by **CSSM-BLAST**, plotted in red. This differential reaches a maximum at about the 50th false positive, after which no new true positives are detected by either method." The audience's attention will go immediately to the noted location.

The speaker would not leave the image until she has clearly stated the spin: "This graph demonstrates that **CSSM-BLAST** detects more true positives when compared to **BLAST**."

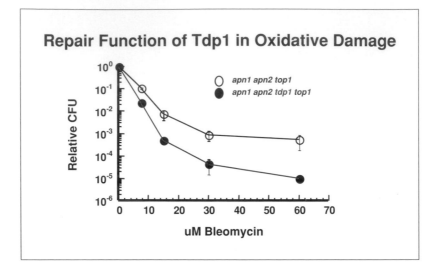

6.2

Here is another example (Figure 6.2) Preview: "We plotted the relative CFU of the two yeast strains, with or without Tdp1 knockout, after treatment with Bleomycin. I've highlighted the Tdp1 knockout in red."

Highlight: "Note the drop in relative CFU beginning almost immediately and continuing through 60 uM of Bleomycin."

Spin: "This indicates that repair of oxidative damage does involve Tdp1."

When there are multiple images to discuss, the speaker can assure that she gives adequate preview by inserting a black slide before each image. The black screen will remind her to introduce the forthcoming image before showing it. An audience benefits from the blank screen as well; they are not distracted by looking at "stale" data while the presenter proceeds to the next step, and they can concentrate on the words between the findings.

The three-step method accomplishes several worthwhile goals. First, it minimizes the visual static that arises when an audience has to choose between several focal points. Second, the technology supports the presentation, not vice versa. Third, there is an unmistakable bounce in the speaker's credibility when the images are introduced first. The speaker appears to have a better grasp of the material and better control over the presentation.

To review, the three-step process to follow for each presented image is:

1. Preview: Describe the image before bringing it onto the screen, as well as any particular area that may require attention first.
2. Highlight: Draw the audience's attention to the part that is most pertinent to the talk.
3. Spin: Relay the significance of the finding.

The Mechanics of Being Heard

In terms of delivery, the public speaker's first duty is to be heard by the audience. Yet it is not uncommon for someone who speaks intelligibly in everyday conversation to sound weak and indistinct when addressing a larger group. Obviously, an audience will not understand what they cannot hear. But a speaker's inaudibility creates an additional problem: An audience often interprets inaudible science as dubious science.

PSYCHOLOGY

There are several factors that determine the degree to which one is heard and understood by the audience. The first is whether one *wants* to be heard. Shyness, nervousness, and/or a lack of confidence in one's work can all make it difficult to present with conviction.

But regardless of how a speaker may feel personally, there are techniques that can help her to be heard. For example, look at the audience, as opposed to lingering on notes, the screen or the floor. Work toward maintaining eye contact with the audience for at least

90 percent of the presentation. Looking at attendees reminds a speaker to talk to them. A presenter might assume that a microphone compensates for a soft-spoken delivery. But the purpose of a microphone is to magnify natural sound, not to create it. A timid, wispy delivery into a microphone will only sound like an amplified timid whisper. Speak out with a full voice to the audience members who are farthest away, whether there is a microphone or not. A common dictum for public speaking is that an audience is like a lawn, and the presenter's job is to water every section of it during performance. Also, thinking of the audience as a whole allows the speaker to observe individual reactions (such as attentiveness or boredom) without taking them personally.

VOCAL TONE

When most of us speak, it is customarily to another individual or to a small group of listeners – that is, in a private rather than a public setting. Talking to a larger audience demands that the speaker approach the *physical* aspects of communication more consciously.

The following drills have been adapted from the techniques of voice teacher Margaret Riddleberger. We have condensed her techniques into a few short exercises that can help with vocal quality and articulation. They do not require a lot of time, but done regularly, can result in significant improvement.

Most vocal problems result from the incorrect assumption that sound is manufactured by the vocal cords. In fact, rich vocal quality comes from releasing air deep in the lungs, which passes effortlessly *through* the vocal cords. It takes a flexible torso to generate as much of this air as possible.

Thus, the first exercise will loosen the lower back, creating more space for the diaphragm. Place both hands on the waist so that the fingertips touch the top of the hipbone, thumbs resting against the lowest rib. Very slowly and gently, extend the torso so that the space between the fingers expands. This motion should be incremental, like the slow opening of an accordion. Stretch up and down several times, silently. Stretch another few times while making a hissing sound ("sss"), and then a few more times with a hum ("mmm"). Only vocalize when the body moves upward and the lungs exhale. This will prevent tension in the throat.

To lengthen and strengthen the middle back, clasp the hands together in front of the chest as if playing volleyball. Keeping them together, slowly raise them overhead. Bend the elbows and try to touch the middle of the back with the thumbs. Make sure the head and back remain straight at all times. Repeat this movement, exhaling each time: without sound, then with a hiss, and then with a hum.

If performed frequently, these exercises will both improve richness of vocal tone and increase natural speaking volume. To apply these techniques during a presentation, maintain a comfortable but fully upright posture. If there is a podium, avoid leaning on it. A straight posture helps generate a strong voice.

DICTION

Contrary to popular belief, an audience's full comprehension of a speaker is not a matter of her vocabulary or accent. Comprehension is highest when she slows down the rate of speech and fully articulates the words. All presenters, whatever their native tongue, could stand to improve the crispness of their diction.

The greatest resonator of sound in the human body is bone. Fortunately, we have been equipped with an interconnected skeletal system, which can function as a personal sound studio. As air travels up from the lungs, it eventually hits the teeth. Here, the air is transformed into vibration and, like electricity, is conducted up through the maxilla, vomer, perpendicular plate, nasal and zygomatic bones and then onto the skull. Any air directed toward the teeth will follow this natural route, avoiding the vocal cords and alleviating tension in the throat. In turn, less tension in the throat allows more air to be converted into vibration. This circuitry produces a resonant sound, unique to each individual speaker.

The quickest way to activate this circuitry is to repeat a few exercises using a plastic straw.

Place the straw (or plastic coffee stirrer) between the teeth and repeat the following sounds: "ah, ay, ee, oh, oo."

As one intones these sounds, there should be no sensation in the throat and only a slight vibration on the lips and the teeth. Now repeat the exercise, adding consonants before the vowels. For example, "nah, nay, nee, no, noo." Repeat again using each of the remaining consonants.

Continue using the straw to say key words or phrases from a talk. Because the straw creates a slight obstacle for the tongue to navigate, the delivery of complicated words becomes slow and deliberate. Now remove the straw and repeat the phrases, while directing the same degree of attention to the front teeth as when the straw was in place. The vibrating sensation should be similar, and every syllable noticeably articulated.

This is a particularly important exercise to perform with any word a speaker uses routinely. She may say "cerebral granular cells" several times a day in the lab, with the resulting tendency to compact the seven syllables into four. This unconscious habit typically carries over to a presentation. And if a word is difficult for the speaker to say, then it is also a difficult word for the audience to understand. So the time devoted to rehearsing important words is time well spent.

Accents and Mannerisms

Presenters are often worried about how they come across *personally* to the audience. This is an understandable concern, because a presentation is in many ways an extension of themselves. Fortunately, their two primary areas of concern, their accents and mannerisms, are less problematic than they usually think.

Regarding accents, non-native English speakers typically have no more difficulty being understood than native English speakers. As long as they have a working knowledge of English scientific vocabulary, the former group may even have a couple of advantages. One is that most audiences find foreign accents delightful to listen to. But the more pertinent reason is that non-native English speakers are probably already aware of potential hurdles to an audience's clear understanding, and may have already made a conscious effort to surmount those obstacles.

There are those individuals whose accent is pronounced enough to warrant special attention. Contacting a speech therapist might be advisable in these rare cases. But before taking this dramatic step, practice the preceding diction exercises.

Native English speakers need to perform them too. If anything, they can be hobbled by the assumption that they are easily understood, simply by virtue of their "unaccented" English. However, they are as likely to compact key words and phrases as anyone else. An American speaker we know once gave an entire talk on the subject of "fishul." After a few minutes the audience was noticeably confused. When he finished, someone asked him what fishul was. "It's not fishul," he replied, "It's fish oil!" Often, it is not the accent that keeps a presenter from being understood, but her lethargy of speech and speed of delivery. The straw exercise can help both native and non-native English speakers slow down and enunciate fully.

Many speakers worry that they will use the wrong word while presenting. Suffice it to say, effective communication is not about getting every word right; it is about conveying the core concepts and the gist of the information. No audience takes offense when a speaker stumbles over a word, or even when she uses an incorrect one from time to time. Nor do they mind occasional pauses as she searches for better ways to express her thoughts.

On the other hand, an audience *is* bothered when a speaker repeatedly loses track of the thoughts themselves. The subsequent tendency is for her to fill the gaps with vocal pauses such as "um," "uh," or "er." A primary cause of repetitive sounds like these is a speaker's fear of silence. Consequently, "um" and "uh" occur as she rushes to fill the void; the result is a seemingly endless run-on sentence. A good first step toward breaking this habit is to rehearse speaking in complete sentences, from period to period, pausing briefly between the sentences. During an actual presentation, it may feel awkward to apply this practice at first, but it effectively removes mid-sentence pauses. The audience, meanwhile, is likely to appreciate the slower pacing and the uncluttered sentence structure.

Some presenters make run-ons worse by stressing too many words inside a sentence. One method of correction is to find the operative word in a phrase and rehearse the sentence aloud using a single emphasis. For example, "Postnatal development of synaptic transmission is mainly based on Calcium Kinetics," might be stressed as follows: "Postnatal development of synaptic transmission is mainly based on *Calcium* Kinetics." This procedure drives the sentence to the most important idea, which is almost always at the end.

To further help tackle the fear of silence, consider an opposing philosophy: Silence actually allows the audience time to absorb what the speaker has just said. Pauses in delivery permit attendees to fill in the gaps by themselves, making them active participants in the presentation process. Silence can become a speaker's valued teaching assistant. The trick is not to fill the quiet, but to allow it to linger a moment.

Most speakers are also self-conscious about their mannerisms: how they move, how formally or informally they should express themselves, what to do with their hands, and so forth. To reduce this self-consciousness, imagine speaking to the audience as though telling a story to a group of friends. When the presenter concentrates on sharing the material, instead of on individual gestures, all her means of expression naturally follow suit.

A Latin American speaker told us that she had been taught to present formally, with her arms at her side or clasped behind her back. As a result, her delivery was flat and boring. After she permitted herself to gesture as she would in ordinary conversation, the sparkle and enthusiasm came rushing back into her presentation.

We have seen countless variations on this theme. There are speakers who favor remaining motionless behind the podium; others use big, sweeping arm gestures. We have even seen a Nobel laureate stride across the stage, impersonating atoms. They all presented very effectively. The lesson is not to copy anyone else's style. If a speaker prefers to remain stationary, then she should do so; if movement feels more natural, that is an equally good choice. Each speaker has a set of mannerisms that when left alone, actually help her convey the information best.

The former British Prime Minister, Benjamin Disraeli, once said, "Every product of genius must be the product of enthusiasm." A presentation is truly infectious when a speaker taps her innate enthusiasm. We are not suggesting that speakers use a wild cheer to whip the crowd into a frenzy or the slick pitch of a car salesman. We are referring instead to the eager sensation of sharing important information and the thrill of imparting new discoveries. This kind of enthusiasm engages the audience and inspires the speaker to teach.

Enthusiasm can be fostered by making a talk the priority of the day. Monitor energy output in the hours preceding a talk, so there is plenty to draw on during the presentation. To give the voice a light workout, make an effort to speak out loud sometime before the presentation; even talking on the phone is helpful. Prior to the talk, take a brisk walk. Just before beginning, remember how vital the information is; then step forward and share it.

What to Rehearse

Once they have prepared a talk, speakers often assume that the best way to rehearse it is to run through it over and over in its entirety. And in fact, rehearsal is a necessary tool to increase confidence and keep nervousness at a productive level. But it helps to be selective in identifying what actually needs repetitive practice.

We have heard many definitions of practice over the years: writing out the whole presentation verbatim, practicing before a mirror, and making an audio or video recording. Having tried all these methods, we can honestly say that none of them work. They only make one feel more self-conscious, while the goal of rehearsal is to make one feel less so.

Perhaps surprisingly, we particularly discourage self-recording with audio or video equipment. Presenters often think they can watch themselves on tape objectively, but it is virtually impossible to do so. During playback, almost everyone becomes obsessed with some part of their appearance: their hair style, clothing, physical features, voice, gestures, and so on. Yet an audience will notice these things only in passing, if at all. A camera cannot capture the audience's subjective experience, which is based in the totality of the presentation. So, a speaker watching a recording of herself will not see the same speaker an audience sees. This kind of feedback essentially takes the speaker "out of context," and she is more likely to make changes to her performance based solely on appearance.

It is more productive for the presenter to remain grounded in her own subjective experience by centering her attention on how the talk feels from her side of the podium. With time and practice, many presenters develop a "sixth sense" that lets them know they are teaching well. This personal perspective is a far more reliable guide for improvement than a recording.

Some presenters do, nonetheless, like to rehearse before a mock audience. In which case, we suggest that they practice before colleagues from a separate department. Because these listeners do not have a working knowledge of the material, they are more likely to point out gaps in the talk's logic, unclear visual aids, and imprecise descriptions.

Before any full presentation or rehearsal, there are only three things that need practice: the major structural signposts, the logical flow of the introduction, and the pronunciation of key words. Polishing these elements in advance will allow for a more clear and spontaneous presentation.

CHAPTER 6 CHECKLIST

- [ ] Assign the "internal critic" the job of speech coach.
- [ ] Practice delivery of key words using the straw exercise.
- [ ] Make teaching the main goal of the talk.
- [ ] Use the three-step process for presenting every slide.
- [ ] Rehearse the key structural components of the talk.

7 FIELDING QUESTIONS

Before I came here I was confused about this subject. Having listened to your lecture I am still confused. But on a higher level.

– Enrico Fermi

Most of our clients report that the Question and Answer Period is as fearsome as giving the presentation itself. Even the kindest question can cause a presenter to scramble for the proper reply, often making him feel silly and self-conscious in the process. Not to mention those less than respectful questions that are the stuff of a speaker's nightmares. All in all, the question and answer session can seem like "open season" on the poor speaker, who may feel prone and vulnerable.

To repeat, that is how the question period can *seem* to be. But while the speaker may be alone, there is no need for him to feel defenseless. Managed well, this part of the presentation can conclude his time "in the spotlight" on a positive, even satisfying note. What follows are a few strategies to increase the odds of a good Question and Answer (Q & A) experience, while protecting the speaker from verbal attack.

Laying the Groundwork for Q & A

There is no need to wait until the questions start flying to deal with them. The speaker can take the first steps toward managing the question period in the talk itself.

Above all, the Main Question must be unmistakably clear. Come Q & A, a clear Main Question sets the parameters for the day's discussion.

As an example, the Main Question, "How does NKD28 inhibit cell interaction in the lipid raft micro-domain?" announces that the talk will center on one thing only: NKD28. The question sends an implicit message that any queries from the audience should revolve around this specific topic. And because it is in the form of a question, it stands out from the Introduction's declarative statements and catches the audience's ear. If the questions threaten to go off track, the speaker simply reminds the audience of the talk's focus. An audience that clearly hears the Main Question will usually stick to the subject.

If an audience member deviates from this subject, the speaker has a choice of whether to answer the less-than-relevant question. He might choose to answer with a short comment: "NKD28 was the topic of discussion today, but the brief answer is . . ." If he chooses not to answer, a polite statement along the lines of, "My focus today was on NKD28, and so as to respect everyone's time, I'll be happy to talk with you at the end of the session," should get the questions back on course.

If the speaker veers too far away from the main subject, it will only invite a wider range of questions during Q & A. So it may be useful to refer to the Main Question at critical junctures in the talk itself.

Using a phrase such as, "This finding brings up a host of interesting issues about the lipid raft domain, but not all are pertinent to our study of NKD28," acknowledges that every related subject cannot possibly be covered in the time allowed – only the one suggested by the Main Question.

Q & A Basics

After closing with a solid Exit Line, the presenter should change his body position relative to the audience. This physical shift signals a transition into the less formal part of the talk. If he has been standing behind a podium during the presentation, he should move to one side or in front of it for the Q & A period. If presenting without a podium, perhaps he could walk toward the edge of the platform, move closer to the audience, or lean against a nearby table. He might raise the light levels in the room, if possible. Any adjustment that indicates the presentation is now a dialogue invites the audience to join in.

Once the questions begin, be sure to repeat each one before answering it. This simple act serves several functions. One, it lets everyone hear the question. In all but the smallest of meetings, invariably someone does not hear the question, so repeating it is actually necessary. (If the group is so small that repeating the question feels foolish, at least ask if everyone has heard properly.) Two, repetition gives the speaker a second or two to formulate an answer. It is surprising how helpful this brief moment can be in wording a response. Three, it reminds the speaker to answer the entire audience, not just the person asking the question. Fourth, the speaker can redirect toward the topic of the talk. Consider using phrases such as, "What I hear you asking is . . ." or, "That actually applies to today's topic in an interesting way . . ." And fifth, question repetition can help shorten a lengthy, multipart question either to its essence or to a series of separate, more manageable questions. For example:

> **QUESTION:** I wanted to ask about the models for schizophrenia development you mentioned. There seems to be evidence for both neurodevelopmental and neurodegenerative development models. And why we should be looking at the place of estrogen in either one is unclear to me. I don't see how looking at estrogen is borne out by the data. What have you found with regard to the matter of which model is most convincing at this point?

> **ANSWER:** I think I hear you asking three questions: Which model is most convincing; why the release of estrogen is appropriate for study; and where the hormone shows up in the actual research. The issue most relevant to my subject today is how the data validates our focus on estrogen. You might recall my third slide, the graph of . . .

Lastly, regarding question repetition, beware of overusing the phrase, "That's a good question." It sounds insincere if used more than once.

Sometimes a question deviates from the topic, yet the speaker decides to field it anyway. The trap is that an off-topic question typically requires that the presenter give significant background to reply to the whole audience. In these cases, be as brief as possible. Long answers are never appropriate. They interfere with the give and take of a good Q & A session, can cause alienation from the rest of the audience, and threaten to overextend the presentation time.

Worst-Case Scenarios

Sometimes a person in the audience will catch a relevant point the presenter neglected to address and will bring it up in front of the entire group during Q & A. When this happens, it is best to acknowledge the gaffe, apologize, and then briefly address the point. As mortifying as this scenario can be to experience, it typically will only happen once. The authors have both been embarrassed in this way; in fact, we can still quote the questions verbatim. Humiliation has a way of searing the forgotten information into one's memory. We never forget to cover the once-overlooked material in every seminar.

Another unpleasant scenario is being stumped by a question. In this case, "I don't know" is a perfectly valid answer. It may feel embarrassing, but it is certainly preferable to giving a long and incomplete answer, which is perceived as evasive. A graceful version of "I don't know" might be, "I'd be happy to discuss that with you afterwards. I'll have to think about it." Any variation of "I don't know" acknowledges that the question has raised a valid point. Not necessarily a pleasurable task, but it shows genuine humility, which audiences appreciate; it also moves the conversation off the uncomfortable topic quickly.

After the session, a speaker will probably formulate a response in case the question arises again. It might even be a point that needs to be permanently added to the presentation.

Then there are the obstinate questioners: those who use Q & A as a personal soapbox for a treatise on their own work, or to spout an oratory disguised as a question. Obviously, Q & A is not the time to get into a heated discussion with a single individual. Give a brief answer and move on to another question. There will be plenty of moral support from the audience, who always (though silently) side with the speaker when a question seems rude or a comment inappropriate. Treating a pseudo-question earnestly but with a short remark is the most professional way to defuse the situation.

Lastly, if there is a host or moderator, do not wait for him to wrap things up. Ultimately, the speaker is in charge of the entire presentation. If there are no more comments or questions, thank the audience for their attendance and close the session.

CHAPTER 7 CHECKLIST

☐ Make the Main Question unmistakably clear.

☐ Repeat all questions.

☐ Give brief answers.

☐ Answer off-topic questions after the session.

At a Glance

1 Have a short and engaging title.

2 Speak with a strong voice and precise diction.

3 Share genuine enthusiasm for the subject.

4 In the Introduction, acknowledge the audience's field of work and knowledge base.

5 Provide a clear focus via a Main Question.

6 Feature one Money Slide among the data, describing it particularly well.

7 Include an appropriate number of Supporting Slides for the time allowed.

8 Teach the audience with ample description of the material.

9 To remain in control of the presentation, exhibit minimal reliance on the images.

10 Preview, highlight and "spin" each image.

11 Encapsulate the data with a brief Take Home Message.

12 Give future directions succinctly, with a specific example for each.

13 End with a strong Exit Line.

14 Repeat each question from the audience and keep answers brief.

15 End the session on (or under) time.

8 THE JOB INTERVIEW

> ... research in pure science leads to revolutions, and revolutions, whether political or industrial, are exceedingly profitable things if you are on the winning side.
>
> – J. J. Thompson, in *J. J. Thompson* by Lord Raylcigh (1943)

Rarely are the skills of public speaking put to greater test than when a job is on the line. In a professional interview, which may include a "job talk," the judges scrutinize the presentation carefully. And the interview questions, which can come at any time, are often the most consequential part of the entire process.

Whether one's career progresses into research, academia or the private sector, the real agenda of the interview is usually below the surface.

It is an accomplishment just to make it to the interview stage. But the frustrating truth is that there is little peace in being short-listed for a job. At this late stage of the interview process, the job panel has evaluated personal statements, letters of recommendation, school transcripts, test scores, and job experience, among other criteria. Yet these factors alone are an insufficient basis for making a final selection. What tips the scales is the information the candidate provides in the interview itself.

What They Will Ask

As much as a candidate would like to divine what the judges think is a "good fit," she can never truly know. The first impressions of the judges are completely out of her control. Surprise questions will always arise. However, there are a few categories of questions common to virtually every job interview. By thinking of answers to them in advance, an applicant can respond more thoughtfully and remain relatively calm through the more predictable parts of the examination.

These questions may appear to be straightforward or to be simply asking the candidate to repeat information from the application. However, the best answers are not the obvious ones.

MOTIVATION/ATTRACTION

Even though the candidate's personal statement is attached to the application, personal questions will still come up during the face-to-face interview. Interviewers need more details than the application allows for; they want to get a sense of the person behind the prepared statements.

Thus, a common interview question is, "What initially motivated you to be a scientist?" or "What attracted you to the field?"

The strongest response to this question is a specific example. If an applicant gives a general answer such as, "I always wanted to be a doctor," it does not reveal anything more profound about her. One client of ours gave a more detailed answer to this question. She recounted how as a teenager, she volunteered to provide medical services to villagers in a third world country. She was so moved by this work that she called her parents to tell them that she wanted to stay there forever. They eventually persuaded her that going to medical school first was perhaps an even better way of helping those underserved.

Another client said that he was inspired to move into the field of CT colonoscopy scanning because, while in medical school, he was impressed with the diagnosis and treatment made possible by computer graphics. "It was exciting to see clear visual images make such a difference in treatment," he said, adding, "No matter how technology evolves, I still get the same thrill."

Instead of a broad statement, then, relay a real-life experience or a brief story that best exemplifies one's attraction to the field or profession. The more detailed and colorful a recollection is, the more impressive the answer will be to the interviewers. A panel is not merely asking whether the applicant is motivated, but how strong that motivation is. Only an honest example demonstrates that strength.

This kind of answer also saves the candidate a lot of stress. She does not have to waste time trying to fashion the "right answer." Nor does she have to worry that the answer is too long or too short; a real-life anecdote begins at a relevant place, goes straight to the point and comes to a natural end. A personal example is so clear in the candidate's mind, she need not comment on it further.

BACKGROUND

A complete resume is included in the application, of course, but it only gives a list of positions, not an account of the most significant ones. In the interview, it is helpful to the judges if the candidate highlights the educational and professional experiences that have been especially meaningful to her. Perhaps it was a special mentor, a certain research tool, or a specific case study that made the greatest impact on her educational or professional development.

> "One of the most rewarding experiences I had was at the National Heart, Lung, and Blood Institute, where I studied mammalian physiology. I was deeply involved in a study about the formation of vesicles and the molecules involved in cell vesicular trafficking. This study also led to the publication of my first paper."

The applicant might also emphasize any previous work with an applicable connection to the employer.

If there is some confusion as to whether the interviewers are asking about professional or personal background, the candidate is fully within her rights to ask for clarification. In the event the question is seeking personal background, the same guidelines about using specific examples apply.

STRONG POINT/WEAK POINT

Questions such as, "What are your strongest and weakest attributes?" come with built-in traps. The "strength" question, for instance, can lead a candidate to make claims that sound arrogant and abstract. An effective answer to this question will instead be simple and factual.

It may be difficult to isolate a professional strong-point trait. For practice, try to identify a personal strength first – for example, "I am a good cook." Then be sure to add why: " . . . because I have a good sense of what food combinations work well together. I pay particular attention to the textures of the ingredients." Using the same thought process, isolate a strong point (however small) that indicates a positive attribute in the scientific realm:

> "I think I work well with students. Currently, I have two technicians working with me, and just the other day one of them came running up to me to say that he had just finished a Northern blot all on his own. That felt great."

"Having worked on transplant composition for six years, I understand in detail how to apply it to research in immune reconstitu-
tion. Sometimes I think I could do it blindfolded."

A variation of the strong-point question is, "Why should we hire
you over the other candidates?" The best answers to this question
reveal not merely the applicant's commitment to her field, but also
her passion for it. They should reflect her genuine love of pursuing
science. It may be helpful to think in terms of one's overall career
rather than the outcome of this particular interview: "Even if I don't
get this job, what keeps me devoted to my field?" An example:

"I have worked for two years studying the transition mechanism of
preinvasive tumors. I put in many hours of my own time, and I am
just now starting to see some results. Even after two years, I still
love the work. I would do it for free."

As for the "weak point" question, the trap is that the applicant
will answer with an apology (for instance: "When I work on my own,
I'm not as productive as I'd like to be") or with false modesty ("My
main flaw is that I am a perfectionist"). She can avoid these traps by
honestly naming a weak point, either professional or personal, and
describing the steps she is taking to overcome it.

For instance, one of our clients first responded to a weakness
question with, "I don't know enough languages." But that response
merely sounded meek; it could be said of practically anyone. Later,
she elaborated: "I actually find learning languages difficult. So I am
making myself speak Hindi with my parents, and I'm taking Spanish
classes on Thursday nights." With this answer, she not only shares
her weakness and what she is doing to correct it, but she also gives
the impression that when she faces a challenge of *any* kind, she
devises a plan of action to confront it.

A more scientifically specific example of a weak-point answer is: "I find scientific writing hard to do. But I'm taking a 12-hour writing course this month to improve my grant proposals."

A straightforward response to a strong-point/weak-point question displays sound judgment and self-awareness. As a result, the job panel will see a candidate who is more likely to be honest with herself and with others.

FUTURE VISION

An interview usually includes questions such as, "Where do you see yourself in five years?" or, "How do you see your career unfolding?"

Phrase these answers in terms of a feasible and practical goal. Avoid the "beauty pageant answer," such as, "I want to cure cocaine addiction." The best response is more tangible and includes specific stages that lead to the final goal:

> "I hope to develop a clinical candidate for cocaine abuse treatment. First, we will need to build up the body of synthetic databases. I'd also want to coordinate with those in other fields so that within five years, we could see a new drug on the market."

CURRENT WORK

In a short interview, there may be only a few seconds for a speaker to describe her current work. In brief conversations such as these, give the Introduction to a talk for a large organization (Figure 4.3). Taken together, Common Ground, background information and the Main Question provide a clear, logical and brief validation of a given study.

In interview situations, if there is even the slightest possibility that someone listening might need a definition, be sure to include it. Often, the person least familiar with the field has the greatest sway in hiring decisions.

For longer interviews, there may be time to include a few data points, the Take Home Message and perhaps even part of the Resolution Section. But any foray into data should be concise. Because there will be no chance to use visual aids, the applicant who verbally describes her work best is likely to make the strongest impression. The best preparation for a discussion of current work is an exercise we call "radio science."

Radio Science

In this exercise, the speaker practices major portions of her talk without showing any visual aids. While rehearsing, she may look at images as a reminder, but she should remember that the audience cannot see these images, just as if she were speaking on a radio program. With Radio Science, it is imperative for the scientist to discuss the data thoroughly and to give the spin of each finding. It will also help if she describes her data in visual terms because she must also serve as the audience's "eyes." Examples:

> "The compounds appear as red and green spots on a black background. When we used the new technique, the red spots increased in size by fifty percent."

> "This receptor looks like a thread, weaving between the plasma membrane and the surrounding cytoplasm."

> "Small RNAs are hook shaped, like a hairpin."

Radio Science forces a speaker to discuss her data points in innovative ways by drawing connections between them via verbal description, rather than through the use of pictures. (As an auxiliary benefit, should the technology ever fail during an actual presentation, she is prepared to continue without images.)

Practice this exercise at least once prior to an interview; and for the reasons mentioned above, before either a standard presentation or a job talk as well.

The Job Talk

Even as she rehearses the description of her data, an applicant will do well to recognize that the data per se is not the interviewers' primary focus. At an earlier point in the application review, interviewers have found that the applicant has compelling data and skillful technique. But as mentioned, they have concluded the same of everyone else on the short list. It is easy to see why data are not an employer's top priority. The applicant's topic is not likely to reflect the same variables used in their own institution, nor is it likely to match their exact research needs.

However, if at every stage in a presentation, the applicant makes the logical course of her research evident to the job panel, this tells the panel something very useful: They only need to plug in a new set of values, and the applicant will apply the same thoughtfulness to their studies. This means that during the presentation they are actually watching the speaker think; they are following not so much what she has discovered, but how she has discovered it. The speaker's internal monologue should be: "Am I being as clear as possible? Is there a more helpful way to describe this step? Is there anything else my listeners need to know before I move to the next point?" A candidate who teaches well, giving the context for the scientific relevance of her study and scrupulously connecting each piece of data to the next, demonstrates her value as a scientist.

It will also help the candidate to draw a link between her work and that of the institution. To find this Common Ground, she may have to conduct a little research first. She might ask questions such as, "What branch will be conducting the interview? What do they do? Where does their funding come from? What are they working on?"

Again, the Introduction worksheet (Figure 4.3) will help determine both the appropriate amount of background and which concepts and terms warrant special description.

An applicant benefits greatly by showing adaptability during the interview. An opportunity to do so is likely to present itself during the question and answer session following a job talk. Interviewers will tend to aim their questions not so much at the data, but toward theoretical and hypothetical issues. This way, the panelists get a better idea about the speaker's inventiveness – her ability to "think outside the box." A good preparatory step is to ponder a few theoretical questions, such as: How would I approach the same research described in my presentation if I were given a new set of variables? How would I proceed if there were no time limitations? What kind of study would I design if money was not an obstacle? A bit of imagination will fuel the best responses.

If the panel asks, "Do you have any questions for us?" the candidate can also choose from the five major categories. She might ask, for instance, "Where do you see the institution going in the next five years?" or "What are the most exciting projects you are working on?"

In a job talk, as in any talk, the speaker who teaches her audience, clearly and succinctly describing each stage of experimentation and drawing connections between successive stages, is likely to leave the best impression.

CHAPTER 8 CHECKLIST

☐ Rehearse specific, personal examples for each of the major categories of interview questions.

☐ Practice speaking about current work using the Radio Science exercise.

☐ Use a teaching tone during the job talk.

9 THE MEDIA INTERVIEW

We don't do science for the general public. We do it for each other. Good day.

> – Renato Dalbecco, the complete text of
> an interview in *The Sciences* (1983)

At one time, scientists thought they worked in a rather secluded realm. They might continue at their work for years without the outside world paying much attention. But now, magazines, newspapers, and television and radio stations are hungry for scientific news. The most unassuming scientist might suddenly find that his subject matter has become a "hot topic" and that the media is pounding at the door for comments and information. In these instances, the scientist will find his speaking skills immediately displayed to the vast public.

No matter what subject reporters are covering, their questions usually boil down to, "What's new in your field?" and "Why is it important?" They are, in other words, coming with essentially the same questions as an audience does for a talk. Consequently, many of the structural tools used in preparing and delivering a presentation are equally useful in this new context.

At the same time, the media interview is an information exchange like no other. The relatively large audience is one obvious difference between a media presentation and the average talk. Another is that in a media interview, one's words are recorded for all time. The way a speaker's words are interpreted and conveyed to the audience is usually not his decision, but someone else's. Then there are the possible ramifications of the interview; for example, a scientist's comments could influence social discussion and public policy, or impact the funding of a particular issue. This combination of high impact and little or no control can make speaking with the media an exciting but risky proposition.

In short, a media interview asks a speaker to deploy familiar presentation components in novel ways. Next we consider some of the practical steps that can enhance the opportunity while minimizing the downside.

The Basics

There are basically two types of media interviews: those for print and those for broadcast. In either medium, two kinds of stories prompt the vast majority of interview requests.

The first is a general or "feature" piece on a given subject: for instance, how the spike protein functions in a host receptor. This kind of article or program is usually quite detailed and may come together over several weeks; the advance notice the speaker can expect is relatively generous.

The second kind is a "news" piece: say, on how research into the spike protein has led to the possible discovery of a new flu vaccine. In these cases, the story will probably be written to a much tighter deadline, and the interview request will be more urgent.

With either type of interview, the speaker's first step is to find out whether his institutional guidelines permit him to correspond directly with the media. In fact, one should take this step immediately upon employment, as a matter of policy. At many institutions, all contact with the media must first be cleared either through public relations, a communications department, or a superior.

There could be many reasons for such strict communication protocol. Those in change of public relations have their own methods for handling requests. Perhaps, unbeknownst to the speaker, they have already prepared a news release on the subject or are planning a press conference. Or they may prefer to shield individual scientists and the organization as a whole. Therefore, always go through the appropriate communication channels established by the institution before responding to a reporter's questions.

Small organizations and new companies may not have a public relations office, a human resources department or even a designated primary media contact. In these cases, it is wise to clear all media communication with a supervisor before agreeing to go on record.

If a scientist grants an interview, there are three cardinal rules to remember: Assume that microphones are always on and tape machines are recording at all times; no correspondence or conversation with a reporter, even the most casual one, is ever "off the record"; and the scientist will rarely see the article, the news clip or even a verbatim transcript before the public does.

These rules mean that a speaker is liable for his comments even if the words are manipulated. But they do not mean that he is helpless.

It is wise and acceptable practice for him to ask the reporter some questions of his own. The first should be, "Who are you with?" Knowing what specific organization the reporter represents may reveal the angle of the story and whether it is sensible for the speaker to participate. For example, he would probably prefer not to be associated with publishers prone to sensationalism.

Good follow-up questions include: "What is your story about?" and "Why are you doing the story now?" The answers will indicate whether the reporter's objective is a feature story or a news piece and what "angle" the reporter wants to take on the subject. A feature story for the medical section of a daily newspaper, for example, will likely take a different approach than a story for a scientific journal.

Another good question is, "Who is your audience for this particular piece?" With this knowledge, the speaker can respond with the appropriate level of scientific detail. Some media outlets are not looking for particulars on the subject, but for short quotations or "sound bites."

Depending on the answers to the previous questions, or for any other reason, the scientist may wish to decline the interview. He might respond, "I'd rather not participate at this time," and/or, "The story is not directly related to my area of expertise." It might also be fitting to suggest someone else who may be of better assistance.

To review the preliminaries, if the speaker wishes to proceed with the interview, he must first:

1. Verify that he is permitted contact with the media.
2. Accept the three cardinal rules of media interviews.
3. Deem the reporter and the news organization reputable.

He can now continue with full awareness of the ground rules.

Some interview requests are spontaneous and require a more rapid decision to participate or not. For example, it is common for reporters to approach a scientist at open meetings or conferences. He is always free in these cases to decline the interview request with a polite, "No comment." And a speaker who would actually like to participate, but needs some time to gather his thoughts, can reply with a statement such as, "I have another commitment at the moment. Could I contact you later in the day?" If he takes this option, then the speaker is committing to the interview and must follow up as promised.

The point is that, as in a question and answer session following a talk, the speaker has the right to feel as comfortable as possible. Some stress may be inevitable during a media interview, but it need not distract from giving clear and concise responses. Nor must his decision to be interviewed revolve solely around the reporter's time schedule.

Whether the speaker is forewarned of the interview or not, there are a few practices that, if performed in advance, can help it go as smoothly as possible.

The best preparation for media interviews is the Radio Science exercise described in Chapter 8. Practicing without visual aids can help a speaker become much more adept at giving media interviews, where no visual aids are available. Radio Science makes the images (and the connections between them) so apparent in the speaker's mind that he describes his data with clearer oral logic.

Getting Ready

If the subject of the interview is a current "hot topic" receiving attention in the media, become familiar with the viewpoint that other publications and news organizations have taken in regard to it. Also, read or listen to other stories by the same reporter. This will give an idea as to how he approaches a subject and how questions are phrased.

Choose a Take Home Message for the interview. Media representatives organize their news stories around a single concept, and a speaker should do the same. Also, a precise Take Home Message becomes more likely to clear the final edit. A key point, reworded and repeated often, can even help shape the story.

Depending on which news organization is conducting the interview, the Take Home Message will vary. For a specialty journal, use a Take Home Message with the same specificity as that used for a presentation to one's peers. For example:

The frequency of p53 mutations is higher in anaplastic astrocytoma than in glioblastoma multiform.[1]

For publications aimed at a broader audience, but which nonetheless have a scientific interest, a good Take Home Message might revolve around a broader scientific application:

The cDNA microarray technique is valuable tool for classifying astrocytoma and glioblastoma cells.

And a non-scientific publication or program will probably be more interested in how the news affects the public's daily lives:

A technique called cDNA microarray is helping us find the causes of lethal brain cancers.

Knowing the type of audience involved helps a speaker decide whether to use primarily scientific terminology, lay language or a combination of the two.

Another important preparation step is to determine at least five secondary, equally succinct points that relate to the Take Home Message. The Supporting Slides, and their relevant data, are a good place to look for these supplementary points. The speaker should

[1] Kato, H., Kato, S., Kumabe, T., Sonoda, Y., Yoshimoto, T., Kato, S., Han, S., Suzuki, T., Shibata, H., Kanamaru, R. and Ishioka, C. (2000). *Clinical Cancer Research*, 6, 3937–3943.

rank them in order of importance, and if time in the interview allows, he may expound on them without straying from the main topic.

In addition, for a television or radio interview, prepare a 30- to 45-second overview of the entire subject under discussion. It will probably resemble the Introduction of a talk delivered to a broader audience. This is a constructive place to begin the interview and get the audience "up to speed." The Main Question, which con cludes the overview, will also help direct the reporter's line of questioning. Without the guidance of a speaker's concise Introduction, reporters might script their own; the result may not be accurate and might even be misleading. Reporters will undoubtedly interrupt the overview from time to time, but this should be expected and actually makes the program sound more conversational.

Lastly, formulate the "worst" question imaginable: the most controversial, the most challenging or the most difficult to answer succinctly. Practicing the answer to this question along with the other preparation steps will help a speaker look and feel more confident.

Television Interviews

TV interviews bring additional sources of pressure. The audience could number in the hundreds of thousands, or even the millions. There is only one chance for the speaker to be clear, as there is no going back; and he may be in awe of television itself.

To relieve some of the strain, here are some helpful hints, starting with the simple and concrete.

Get plenty of rest the night before. Do not over-caffeinate before the interview, and save any heavy exercise until afterward.

Dress conservatively; semiformal business attire usually creates the best impression. Men should wear a coat and tie (the tie can always be removed for a more casual look) and women should wear a business suit with minimal jewelry. Mid-range colors, such as pinks, greens and especially blues flatter the speaker. Avoid bold colors and busy patterns. White fabrics glow too brightly; black absorbs too much light. It is always a good idea to carry a second wardrobe option.

Arrive early at the studio or location site and check in with the point of contact. In most TV studios, there is a waiting room for visiting speakers.

In the event there is not a makeup person on site, women should wear everyday makeup. Men should carry any generic brand of colorless powder; this will dampen any shine caused by the hot lights.

Once the speaker is called to the interview area, a sound technician will place a microphone on the speaker's wardrobe. Do not adjust it for any reason. Its placement is solely the technician's responsibility, and nothing can be done to help should it fall off during the interview.

If the segment is taped and edited before being shown to the public, it is common for reporters to ask a speaker to spell his name and give his title.

Look only at the reporter for the entire length of the interview. The reporter may look at and address the camera, but the scientist should not.

During the interview, keep the answers as accurate and concise as possible. Stick to the Take Home Message and supporting points. Reporters are often listening to a producer through a small ear device; thus, they occasionally repeat all or part of an earlier question. In these circumstances, rephrase the appropriate answer and lead, or "bridge", into one of the supporting points.

The most common worry about appearing on television is what a speaker should do with his hands. There is no perfect solution, because we all use our hands differently and each person should strive to maintain as much "naturalness" in front of the camera as possible. The rule of thumb is for him to use his hands as he would if discussing his work with guests at the dinner table. This ensures an appropriate amount of arm movement and that his hands stay within the picture frame. Locking his hands on the table or in his lap only makes him look rigid.

Whereas we discourage the practice of beginning a talk with statistics, reporters are often eager to hear them, so memorize the key numbers pertaining to the subject: the number of people affected or the amount of funding needed, for example. For clarity's sake, use no more than two key numbers per interview. Even the most important figures may otherwise get lost.

A reporter might quote other researchers who oppose the speaker's methods or findings. The best counter-approach is to maintain focus on the work itself, not on the controversies or personalities involved. As the economist and Nobel laureate, Herbert A. Simon said, "When theories and facts are in conflict, the theories must yield." By focusing on the facts in his research, the scientist takes a big step toward defusing a contentious topic.

Likewise, a reporter may ask for a personal opinion from the speaker. It is shrewd to avoid sharing personal beliefs because the scientist is representing not only himself but also his employer and his organization.

At times there may be silences during the interview. Although the pauses may be awkward, learn to accept them; it is not the responsibility of the guest speaker to make the program go quickly or smoothly.

Be prudent when discussing the possible ramifications of the work. Reporters may hope to uncover news of a major breakthrough, but it is up to the scientist to maintain a sense of perspective.

Rephrase negative responses in the affirmative. Instead of, "We didn't get the results we were hoping for," respond with, "The results pointed us in a new direction." Imagine that the listening audience is made up of grant administrators and stress the positive without exaggeration.

The Inner Critic section of Chapter 6 is particularly helpful in reducing the stress of an on-camera interview. With all the chaos associated with appearing on television, it is imperative that a speaker's own self-criticism not become an additional distraction.

When the interview ends, remain seated, looking at the reporter, but do not stand up until the crew says the interview is over. The microphone needs to be removed and the speaker should not get in the way of the crew setting up for another segment. The staff will probably say good-bye and/or thank you, but it is not an affront to the scientist if they do not.

Follow-Up

Even when the interview goes well, retain a realistic expectation about the final result. Journalists can make errors in reporting and writing; or perhaps the scientist misspoke. Whatever the cause, it is not uncommon for a story to contain incomplete information or even misinformation. If the error is serious enough to warrant a correction, a letter to the editor (for a print interview) or the producer (for broadcast) is the best rejoinder. Point out what was good about the piece as well as its flaws. The letter should be written promptly, while the news is still fresh in everyone's mind. It may not be printed or read on the air, but it will serve as an official rebuttal, and the scientist will know he has done his part to correct the record.

Once a scientist has appeared in the media, he may be contacted for interviews more frequently. With thorough preparation and a confident attitude, he can use media interviews as a great opportunity to describe his work to an ever-widening audience.

CHAPTER 9 CHECKLIST

☐ Confirm institutional procedures regarding media interviews.

☐ Before the interview, isolate a Take Home Message and at least five supporting points.

☐ Prepare a 30-second introduction.

☐ Rehearse answers to the toughest possible questions.

☐ Practice the Radio Science exercise.

☐ Stress the positive aspects of the work.

☐ Swiftly correct any errors in writing.

10 MAKING CLEAR POSTERS

It is the weight, not the number of experiments that is to be regarded.

– Sir Isaac Newton

As irresistible as it may be for a speaker to pack a lot of information into a short talk, the temptation is equally great when creating a poster. A presenter may think that a poster's modest dimensions cannot hold nearly enough data to explain her research. Her tendency, then, is to reduce the font of the text and the size of the images to compensate for the poster's spatial limits. The result is a forbiddingly detailed poster that few people will bother to examine. If a major challenge with a talk is time, then that for a poster is space.

Before tackling this spatial challenge, it is worth considering a poster's primary purpose: to facilitate networking with those in attendance. It should act as a springboard for interaction with other scientists, potential employers and peers. A poster can also open avenues for future discussion, thereby building personal and professional connections long after the poster session has ended. The success of a poster depends on how well it accomplishes these goals.

Organizing a Poster

A poster should attract the attention and curiosity of passersby, enticing them to stop and investigate further. Yet a poster cannot stand alone. Once it draws attention, the presenter is then in charge of illuminating its contents. Therefore, the function of the poster is to support the presenter's verbal description. The components of the Hour Glass Format can also help lay the groundwork for a dynamic poster. The key signpost here, however, is the Money Slide.

The first step in creating the poster is to isolate this image, the one that best represents the work. It can be placed anywhere on the poster, but should be printed 15 to 20 percent larger than the other images. This arrangement not only better attracts viewers and enhances compositional flow, it also accentuates the most significant finding during demonstration.

The second step is to find images that best support the Money Slide. Aim for a maximum of five figures that will cover approximately two-thirds of the poster. After following the suggestions of good slide design proposed in Chapter 3, print the images on a light-colored background so that they stand out clearly.

This configuration will leave about a third of the poster space available for text. Chapter 3 also discusses the dangers of using text-heavy slides within a presentation, and the same dangers apply here. The entire poster should be clearly discernable from five feet away, the depth of two rows of attendees.

In contrast, some presenters believe that including long paragraphs of text and a multitude of images will adequately substitute for a missing presenter. But most viewers will pass by an unattended, text-packed poster in favor of a simpler, attended one. A poster is

Title

Authors

1 Introduction Background Main Question	4 Data & Findings	7 Data & Findings
2 Methods & Materials	5 Data & Findings	8 Conclusions Take Home Message
3 Data & Findings	6 Data & Findings	9 Future Studies Citations and Acknowledgements

10.1

incomplete without explanation; even when the author is present, viewers want her to explain and elaborate on the contents.

In practice, make such text blocks as "Background" and "Materials and Methods" as brief as possible. The key is not to use full sentences. Bullet points are a better choice, for several reasons: They are much easier to read at a glance; they use fewer words, so they can also be printed in a larger font; and they more economically convey the gist of the work, allowing the speaker to extemporize more freely.

In terms of poster layout, the sequence of panels should be placed in vertical columns (as in Figure 10.1) instead of horizontal rows. This means that regardless of the computer software program used to generate the poster (PowerPoint, Adobe, etc.) the first item should be in the upper left hand corner, with the second one immediately below it. This format allows attendees to walk down an aisle of posters without having to backtrack to see all the material.

As a reminder, one of the data blocks in Figure 10.1 would be the Money Slide and therefore would be slightly larger than the others.

Notice that the abstract is missing from Figure 10.1. The abstract may be a required element for the initial submission of a poster (and may be printed in the program booklet), but it makes for boring poster material. If the hosting organization insists that a printed abstract be attached to the poster, make it as brief as possible or refrain from using full paragraphs, opting for bullet points instead.

The sheer number of posters at a typical conference makes it impossible for viewers to visit them all. A presenter must do everything feasible to make her poster stand out. And what typically attracts viewers is the title. As noted in Chapter 5, talk titles are best when kept brief; similarly, shorten poster titles by using colons to separate the main title from the subtitle. Always use the largest font that will fit in the space available. Do not use full caps, such as, "A MANUAL FOR CREATING CLEAR PRESENTATIONS," nor sentence case: "A manual for creating clear presentations." The preferable method is title case: "A Manual for Creating Clear Presentations." However, some meetings may have strict rules regarding title fonts that would supersede these suggestions.

Print the names of the authors in a smaller font size than that of the title. Each author's position and/or degree should be kept to a minimum length, so as not to clutter the overall look of the poster. Among the list of authors, it is helpful for viewers to see the presenter's name underlined or in bold.

For observers who want printed material about the research, provide either an 8.5″ × 11″ copy of the poster or a handout of the highlights with a few pertinent images. A low-resolution digital version will also come in handy as an email follow-up. In all cases, be sure to include contact information.

Conducting the Session

Do not underestimate the potential for networking and meeting employers at poster sessions. Research projects, job prospects, and careers can get a real boost from these presentations. But because it is difficult to tell who among the sea of attendees may be most consequential, it is helpful to think of poster sessions as more of a social gathering, like a cocktail party.

It is as if dozens of guests are arriving at the presenter's house and she has only a few minutes to greet each one before they get lost in the party. In response, make sure that everyone who visits the poster gets a lot of eye contact. If new guests arrive in the midst of the description, kindly smile at them and continue with the discussion, rather than start over again. If a few viewers leave during the explanation, resume eye contact with those who remain and continue with the storyline. The conversation should ideally flow without interruption.

As when hosting a party, be attentive to the guests' needs during a poster session. First, because it is disconcerting for attendees to have to look up at the poster to discover who they are talking to, wear a name tag. Be sure to carry one to the conference in case none are provided.

Second, remain standing during the poster session. These gatherings can be marathons for presenters, but nonetheless, it looks unprofessional to be seated when interested people come by. Even under these trying conditions there are still ways to keep from feeling fatigued. Stay limber by walking slowly in front of the exhibit;

bend the knees slightly or stretch the torso (for details, see "The Mechanics of Being Heard" in Chapter 6). Even minor movement can help a speaker look and feel alert.

Have plenty of business cards on hand as well. Because networking is the main point of the session, give cards to those who show particular interest. Leave business cards in plain view on those rare occasions when the booth is unattended.

Finally, wear attire that is either equal to or, to be safe, one step more formal than that of the guests. If attendees tend to wear jeans, wear khakis; if they wear khakis, wear a jacket; if they wear a jacket, then wear a suit. Dressing professionally conveys respect for the conference as well as for one's colleagues.

For poster examples, see Appendices 2 and 3.

CHAPTER 10 CHECKLIST

☐ Sequence the poster in vertical columns.

☐ Enlarge all pictures, particularly the Money Slide.

☐ Minimize the amount of text by using bullet points.

☐ Create a short and engaging title.

☐ Dress professionally.

☐ Carry plenty of business cards and follow up with interested attendees.

IN CLOSING

> Our ideas are only intellectual instruments which we use to
> break into phenomena; we must change them when they have
> served their purpose, as we change a blunt lancet that we have
> used long enough.
>
> – Claude Bernard

We have witnessed hundreds of speakers both present
more clearly and feel more confident when they follow the preceding guidelines. Good speakers all have similar traits. They draw a
connection between their scientific work and the work of the audience. They introduce concepts and definitions before focusing on
the more detailed aspects of the talk. Like effective teachers, good
speakers logically present the data, and the thoughts behind the
data, so that the audience learns the entire scientific process. Good
speakers have a main theme, which is followed throughout the presentation and is encapsulated in a brief and memorable statement
near the end. They use images to help the audience visualize data,
yet they know that the pictures must always remain secondary to
clear description. They share future plans and finish the presentation on a strong note. Good speakers do all of the above while sharing
their ideas with enthusiasm.

But there is a caveat to the techniques described in this book: They need not be followed all at once. In fact, in the early stages of one's speaking career, they may work best when applied gradually. We recently ran into a former student who said, "I don't remember everything you taught me, but to this day I am very selective about using text slides." As her comment suggests, it is not a set of rules or a list of terms that make a good speaker, but the commitment to improve with each presentation. Perhaps a few of our ideas have been of use already; we hope that others will be in the future.

Great teachers are impressive because they possess vast knowledge about highly intricate subjects. But they are truly extraordinary when they can make complicated things seem simple. The job of a speaker is very similar and equally worthwhile: to make complex ideas clear.

APPENDIX 1

FULL INTRODUCTIONS

Example 1: For the Laboratory Audience

The enzyme Tdp1 is considered to be responsible for repairing damage to topoisomerase 1. Its substrate in this damage is 3′ trapped DNA. The substrate in oxidative damage is also 3′ trapped DNA.

This made us wonder: Is Tdp1 also functional in the repair of oxidative damage?

Example 2: For a Departmental Audience

We now have clear evidence of antiidiotype immune responses in patients with follicular lymphoma, following vaccination with our idiotype vaccine. Despite this, we continue to see some cross-reactive antiidiotype immune responses in our in vitro assays.

To demonstrate that our idiotype vaccine truly has clinical efficacy, we have to demonstrate at least two important points. First, that in these patients who receive the idiotype vaccine, we see some improvement in their disease status, in terms of either shrinkage or complete resolution of their disease. And number two, in those patients where we actually see some change or improvement in their disease status, we can correlate that with some specific antiidiotype immune responses.

With regard to the first point, we have been able to demonstrate something significant in newly diagnosed patients with follicular lymphoma. These patients have undergone conventional chemotherapy, have some molecular evidence of residual disease, and have received our vaccine therapy. We have now demonstrated that they have been able to achieve a molecular remission in some cases, but only after they received the idiotype vaccine.

Regarding the second point, we have been able to isolate the immune cells in some patients following vaccine therapy. In our in vitro lab tests, we have been able to show that these immune cells can recognize the patient's own idiotype protein. In some cases, the cells are only able to recognize the patient's own idiotype protein; in other cases, cells are able to recognize other patients' idiotype proteins.

To actually show that this immune response is specific, not only do we have to demonstrate that the immune cells recognize the patient's own idiotype protein, but also that they recognize *only* the patient's idiotype and not some irrelevant, or other patient's idiotype protein.

Therein lies the problem. Can we find a more specific immunological target to resolve these cross-reactive immune responses?

Example 3: For a Professional Meeting

NK cells are a very important component in innate immunity. They spontaneously kill targets, such as tumor or infected cells. The activation of NK cells is mediated by the balance of activation receptors and the inhibitory receptors on their surface.

However, the recognition of certain class-I MHC molecules by natural killer cells may result in the delivery of an inhibitory signal to the NK cell, which prevents target cell lysis. This inhibition can be overcome by blocking it with antibodies or specific peptides against either MHC or NK cell receptors. Therefore, identification of the residues that are involved in the interaction between inhibitory receptors and their ligands is very important.

The most-studied NK inhibitory receptor is Ly49A. Its ligand H-2Dd and the crystal structure indicate that there are two contact sites: Site 1 and Site 2.

Which site is more important in the interaction of Ly49A and H-2Dd?

What is the overall aim of the lab or branch?

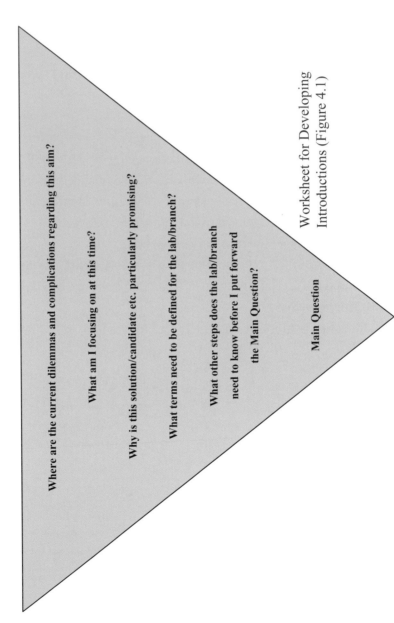

Where are the current dilemmas and complications regarding this aim?

What am I focusing on at this time?

Why is this solution/candidate etc. particularly promising?

What terms need to be defined for the lab/branch?

What other steps does the lab/branch
need to know before I put forward
the Main Question?

Main Question

Worksheet for Developing
Introductions (Figure 4.1)

What is the goal of the department?

What is the overall aim of our branch and/or lab?
Where are the current dilemmas and complications regarding this aim?

What am I focusing on at this time?

Why is this solution/candidate etc. particularly promising?
What terms need to be defined for the department?

What other steps does the department
need to know before I put forward
the Main Question?

Main Question

Worksheet for Developing
Introductions (Figure 4.2)

What is the purpose of the organization or the objective of the professional meeting?

Within this context, what does our institution do?

What is the overall aim of our department, branch and/or lab?
Where are the current dilemmas and complications?

What am I focusing on at this time?
Why is this solution/candidate etc. particularly promising?
What terms need to be defined for the organization?

What other steps does the organization

need to know before I put forward

the Main Question?

Main Question

Worksheet for Developing
Introductions (Figure 4.3)

APPENDIX 2

POSTERS

Real Time Reverse Transcription PCR Quantitation of Anthrax Toxin Expression

Jennifer A. Cockrill, Aaron M. Firoved, Stephen H. Leppla

National Institute of Allergy and Infectious Diseases, National Institutes of Health, Bethesda, Maryland 20892

Introduction

Bacillus anthracis, a gram positive spore forming rod, is the causative agent of anthrax disease. Anthrax toxin is believed to be the main cause of pathologic lesions during infection. Anthrax toxin is composed of three proteins: protective antigen, lethal factor, and edema factor which are encoded by the genes *pagA*, *lef*, and *cya* respectively. *In vivo* expression levels of the three toxin components are currently not known.

Objective

The purpose of this experiment is to establish an in vitro system as a first step toward determining when, where, and in what ratios the three toxin components are expressed during infection.

Materials and Methods

- Attenuated *B. anthracis* AMES (ANR-1) was grown in 50mL LB with 0.8% bicarbonate for 1-2 hours. 1mL was inoculated into 50mL fresh LB with 0.8% bicarbonate and grown at 37 °C, 250rpm with 5% CO₂ to induce toxin expression.
- RNA was extracted at OD₆₀₀ =0.9 and 2.0 using RiboPure-Bacteria isolation kit (Ambion, Austin, TX).
- Primers for reverse transcription PCR were resuspended to 5uM working stock.
- Control oligonucleotides corresponding to PCR amplicon products were used to generate a standard curve from 10⁵-10 copies per reaction.
- Probe was used at a concentration of 1.5uM.
- Real time reverse transcription PCR was optimize d for three primer sets (gyrB) and three toxin genes (cya, lef, and pagA) using Applied Biosystem's taqman1 step RT-PCR mastermix in an ABI 7000 (Applied Biosystems, Hayward, CA).

RNA Extraction Points

Growth Curve *B. anthracis* ANR-1

RNA was extracted from an OD₆₀₀ of 0.9 and 2.0.

Real Time PCR

Forward primer — Probe — MGB

Primer and Probe Sets

Gene Forward primer (+), AntisensePrimer (-),Probe (P)

gyrB
(+) 5'-GGG AATAGT GAA GCG AGA AGA A-3'
(-) 5'-CGT GCAAGG TTC GGG TTT-3'
(P) 6 FAM -ACA GAG TCT GTG TTT-MGB

cya
(+) 5'-GGG GAAGTG CAA ATA AAT CAT AGT C-3'
(-) 5'-ATTGGA ATA TAG T AG AAT TGG TGTGTA AA-3'
(P) 6 FAM -CTG TTA ACG GCT TCA AGA-MGB

lef
(+) 5'-AATGGAGAA TCC ANTAT CAC CAG A-3'
(-) 5'-TTT CCAGAC CGA TGT TTC TTT G-3'
(P) 6 FAM -CTCGAG CAG GAT ATT TAG-MGB

pagA
(+) 5'-AGTGCATCG GTC GTT CTG-3'
(-) 5'-GAA TGATCA ATT GGG ACC GTA CT-3'
(P) 6 FAM -ATA TTG GTG GGA GTG TAT-MGB

Primer Optimization
using 10³amplicons per reaction

*Nanomolar values refer to concentration of primers
* NTC = No template control

gyrB

cya

lef

pagA

Experimental RNA Data for *gyrB* plotted with amplicon standard curve

Total experimental RNA was 120.25ng.

Conclusions

- Primer concentration of 50nM gave sub-optimum amplification. Primer concentration of 900nM gave amplification equivalent to that of 300nM.
- Total RNA isolation is sufficient for amplification int this system.
- An accurate standard curve is generated at the upper range(10⁵-10⁵) but is not defined at lower copy numbers.
- Amplification of no template controlsis present in primer optimization for every gene and is presumably due to contamination by amplicons and/or labconstructs.
- Amplification of the no the template controls limits sensitivity of the assay these by limiting the range of RNA that can be used.

Summary and Future Work

- Issues concerning unexplained amplification of NTCs must be addressed before any data in the lower range can be collected.
- Realtime reverse transcription PCR must be setup in a non-contaminated area using extreme cautionso as to avoid contamination of both reagents and wells.
- Experimental RNA extracted from cultures will be analyzed for transcription.
- System will be used with infections of eukaryoticcells and eventually applied to murinemodels.

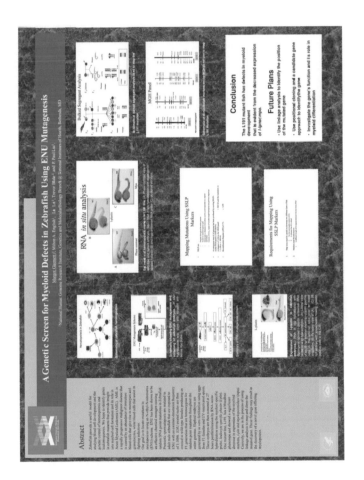

INDEX